PUTTING ON THE GLITZ

OTHER BOOKS AVAILABLE FROM CHILTON

Are you interested in a quarterly newsletter about creative uses of the sewing machine, serger, and knitting machine? Write: *The Creative Machine, PO Box 2634, Menlo Park, CA 94026.*

PUTTING ON THE GLITZ

UNUSUAL FABRICS & THREADS FOR QUILTING AND SEWING

SANDRA L. HATCH
ANN BOYCE

CHILTON BOOK COMPANY
RADNOR, PENNSYLVANIA

Published in Radnor, Pennsylvania 19089, by Chilton Book Company

No part of this book may be reproduced, transmitted or stored in any form or by any means, electronic or mechanical, without prior written permission from the publisher

Designed by Rosalyn Carson

Drawings by Bracey

Other drawings by Ken Tate

Computer drawings by Rosalyn Carson and Sandra Hatch

Photos, except as noted, by Lee Phillips or Charles R. Hatch

Manufactured in the United States of America

Library of Congress
Cataloging-in-Publication Data

Hatch, Sandra L.
Putting on the glitz/Sandra L. Hatch,
    Ann Boyce.   p.   cm. — (Creative
    machine arts series) Includes biblio-
    graphical references and index.
    ISBN 0-8019-8018-6
    1. Machine sewing.
    2. Textile fabrics. 3. Fancy work.
I. Boyce, Ann.   II. Title.   III. Series.
TT713.H36 1990
646.2'044—dc20   90-55316
                                CIP

1 2 3 4 5 6 7 8 9 0   9 8 7 6 5 4 3 2 1 0

ACKNOWLEDGMENTS

There are always many people to thank when a book is written. Many times we read this type of acknowledgment and don't realize how heartfelt the feelings are. The companies below sent us supplies to experiment with. We appreciate their support. They made it easy for us to cover a broad range of sewing experiments. We hope our efforts ultimately will inform and help our readers use the wonderful and varied products available.

Alexander Henry/Central Textiles
Arts International
Bernina of America
Black & Decker
C. M. Offray & Son, Inc.
Coats and Clark
Concord House
Daynell
Dorr Wool Store
Dritz
Elna, Inc.
Fairfield Processing Corp.
Hyman Hendler (Los Angeles)
J.B. Martin Velvets
Lello Appliances Corporation
Madeira, USA
New Home Sewing Machine Co.
Pfaff American Sales Corp.
Plaid Industries
Rhode Island Textile Co.
Rosebar/J&R Interfacings
Singer Sewing Co.
Springmaid
Sulky of America
Swiss-Metrosene
Therm-O-Web, Inc.
VIP Fabrics
VWS, Inc.
Wyla/Weiner Laces
YLI Corp.—Dan Randall and
    Elizabeth Coleman

CONTENTS

FOREWORD

In 1978 the company I work for, Fairfield Processing Corp., began sponsoring a yearly fashion show of wearable art. We link nationally famous designers with the fabric and pattern manufacturers. The resulting Fairfield Fashion Show is introduced to eager quilters and sewers at the Houston Quilt Market each fall.

Over the years, the fashion show has become more and more sophisticated. The garments have become more tailored and intricate and the designers have moved away from using just 100% cottons into lamés, corduroys, velvets, and such. The addition of beads, piping, and metallic threads calls for a solid understanding of fabrics, threads, and the sewing machine.

Predictably, as quilters and sewers want to reproduce what they find exciting, we're seeing more wearable art on the floor and not just on the runway. But handling unfamiliar fabrics is more of a challenge than piecing the traditional cottons. Quilters and sewers need a guide to glitz.

I can't think of two people better suited to write this needed book. I first met Ann in 1984 at the Vermont Quilt Festival. She had heard about the Fairfield Fashion Show and wanted to show me some of her garments. I was immediately excited about the different look to her clothing. At that time, calico patchwork was the traditional embellishment of wearable art. Ann, though, was using all kinds of shiny, glitzy fabrics and threads.

I've known Sandra a long time, too, because as a quilt editor, she's always been interested in our fashion show. I've been impressed with the quality of her editorial coverage in the magazines. She's been on top of the latest movements and was an early, enthusiastic supporter of Ann's style.

The book is even better than I expected. It's a wonderful primer for getting started and working with unusual fabrics and embellishments. Too often people tackle projects without a basic understanding of the fabrics involved. But with this easy-to-follow, well-organized book, you will learn how to avoid potential problems—and how to fix them if you invent some new ones.

I particularly like the way Ann and Sandra have freely shared their expertise. They hold nothing back. I learned lots of tricks of the trade from this book.

I hope reading this book will inspire you to take a step beyond the comfortable. The book shows you how to use what you already know, how adding just a bit of glitz to enliven a quilt, to enhance ready-to-wear, or to update a look will open up a whole new world. Challenge yourself!

Donna Wilder
Director of Marketing
Fairfield Processing Corp.

PREFACE

NOTE FROM ANN

As a free-lance teacher and designer in the quilting and sewing industry, I have discovered many quilters and sewers do not know how to handle and use difficult or unusual fabrics and threads. Because I specialize in using sewing-machine techniques, I am constantly challenged with using my machines to add embellishments that previously could be done only by hand. Most of today's home sewers are trying to balance a career, home, and hobbies—we need to make optimum use of our time. With all the technological advances in the sewing machine industry, we now have machines that can stitch as never before. Many people own these machines, but don't take advantage of their capabilities.

Despite all the fabrics, threads, and trims available today, information on how to sew them has been lacking, but we hope to tie it all up in one neat package in this book. Claire Shaeffer's recent book, titled *Claire Shaeffer's Fabric Sewing Guide* (Chilton, 1989), is a bible on how to sew many fabrics. Our book is devoted to handling unusual fabrics and threads. It is for home sewers who want to go beyond making a simple garment out of one fabric or making a cotton quilt. We want to help you sew more creatively and help you work out the problems that arise when using unusual products so you won't need to struggle.

For the most part, unusual fabrics, trims, and threads are more costly than a home sewer is accustomed to. Our book—which covers a wide variety of techniques on handling fabrics, sewing machine techniques, and finishing touches—should take the cost risk out of being creative. We hope that it will inspire you to venture into new areas of sewing.

NOTE FROM SANDRA

When I took a job editing several quilting magazines and working from my home, I went from working with 120 students a day in my home economics classes to working most days on my own. I didn't have to watch what 25 pairs of hands were doing . I only had to keep myself out of trouble. Along came computers, and my life changed again. With the wonderful programs available, I had fun designing pieced quilt patterns and duplicating them over and over to see how they worked.

Some of these designs could have used a little glitz to make them shine or some beads for embellishment. But how to work with these unusual fabrics, threads, and trims? I had seen a myriad of garments and quilts to inspire me, especially viewing the Fairfield Processing Fashion Show at the Houston Quilt Festival each year. I wanted to expand my horizons but didn't want to spend the time or the money to create something that wasn't really in my repertoire of talents.

Then Ann Boyce moved nearby. She was my antithesis. She was daring where I was not. She could make a quilt from her own design in several days—in fact, she was paid to do so. Thus the beginning of this collaboration.

Although we both learned to sew on our grandmother's treadle machines, Ann could make her machine do things I didn't know sewing machines could do. She was using the latest technology in sewing machines. I was still using Old Faithful.

I watched Ann as she worked, asking constant questions. Our book was born from these questions—questions about the sewing machines, fabrics, and more. Ann and I discussed putting together a book which would answer those and other questions as we discovered new things. Ann would be the resource; I would be the catalyst.

The results are in this book. I have broadened my horizons and found what I like and what I don't like to work with. So will you. As you read and work through this book, you will discover techniques and materials you may want to pursue. Your creative surges will go further than ever before as you try new things. You won't have to experiment because we have done most of that for you.

You will realize that sewing has come a long way from the treadle machines our mothers and grandmothers used, yet they are much the same. The needle still goes up and down, pulling threads from the top and bottom together to make a stitch. The types of stitches and the powering of the machine have changed, but the basics are still the same. Much the same is true for you and me and for Ann, too. We all have some basic talents that result in projects that are stitched together. How those stitches are made is what separates us. Working with unusual fabrics and embellishments can make your work more distinctive and unique.

Enjoy *Putting on the Glitz* and don't be afraid to take a few risks. Who knows what the results will be? But as long as you enjoy yourself along the way, we know you will be happy.

INTRODUCTION

A GROWING TREND

Have you noticed the growing trend among sewers and quiltmakers to put sparkle and glitz into their work by using a variety of fabrics, threads, and embellishments?

In wearable-art fashion shows and quilt exhibits, we are seeing the use of lamés, silks, laces, beads, sequins, and piping. Some sewers add patchwork panels or appliqué accents to ready-made or home-sewn garments or quilts. Others embellish the background with buttons, beads, trims, or metallic threads, to add a sparkling surprise.

The modern sewing machine has made all this possible. Appliqué and piecing can be done by machine instead of by hand. In fact, some machine techniques make it difficult to tell whether the work was done by hand or by machine and they save a lot of time.

Yet with this growing interest, we discovered a real need for a book to cover how to work with these unusual fabrics, threads, and embellishments. Do you need to interface them? Preshrink them? What's the best batting? How does a beginner to glitz plunge in? Where do you buy these supplies?

HOW TO USE THIS BOOK

Based on Ann's vast experience with modern techniques and materials and Sandra's more traditional viewpoint, we decided to write a book to answer these questions. The first chapter tells you what you need to put on the glitz in your own work—equipment and supplies, threads and interfacings. It also discusses options for machine quilting. Chapter 2 covers your choices in clothing and quilt design, pattern selection, and fabrics. Chapter 3 shows you how to apply such embellishments as shisha mirrors, beads, trims, and piping. The final chapter suggests two projects using what you've learned—patchwork on a garment and a modern quilted wall hanging.

SHOPPING

Finding glitz is not difficult. Currently there is a seemingly endless supply of all types of fabrics, trims, buttons, and thread. If you can't find it locally, you can mail order (see our Source List at the end of the book). You can also find unusual items at flea markets, auctions, and antique shops. When you are looking for an accent, you don't need much fabric to make a statement. Sometimes one-quarter yard is just enough to add texture, color, and glitz to the background fabric. Or, if no unusual fabrics are used, you can embellish a background piece with buttons, beads, trims, and several kinds of thread.

GLITZ HISTORY

Using unusual fabrics in quiltmaking is nothing new. In the late fifteenth century, chintz fabrics were introduced to Europe as trade items. Some of the early chintzes arriving in England from India were already quilted whole-cloth quilts.

When the English came to America, they did not forget the chintz fabrics they had known and loved in England. They imported these fine fabrics, and, as time went by, they began to manufacture chintz in America. Thousands of yards were imported or manufactured in the United States between 1775 and 1875. These fabrics opened up a new frontier to the quiltmakers beyond their accustomed fabrics. In the early nineteenth century, manufacturers printed chintz designs especially to be used in making quilts; not only as whole-cloth quilts, but as appliquéd quilts, too. The motifs printed on this chintz—florals, birds, and animals—were cut out with seam allowances and appliquéd onto a background fabric by hand. These quilts were more simple to appliqué than designs made up of individual cut-out pieces.

Examples of this type of quiltmaking survive today and are called "broderie perse." Today we use similar techniques using preprinted panels and fabrics.

QUILTS AND CLOTHING

Quilts and clothing were also made in other fabrics. During the Victorian era, frugal Americans used scraps of silks, taffetas, brocades, and velvets. Even the ribbons tied around cigars and cigarettes were used in quilts. In most cases, these fabric scraps were stitched to muslin squares and sewn together to create a quilt top. Most often the edges of the pieces were hand-embroidered with fancy stitches, and decorative motifs were embroidered on center portions of some pieces. For the most part, these tops were not quilted, but only backed and tied. We see the results of this type of work in the crazy quilts remaining from that era. We also see that these fabrics did not withstand the wear and tear needed by useful items of that period. Some of the fabrics have become brittle and delicate. Simple handling further damages already delicate fibers. Because of this age-old popularity, we have included a section on working with velvets, satins, and silks in this book (Chapter 2). Some good hints for accurately cutting and sewing these somewhat difficult fabrics should help dispel any fears you might have of working with them.

Early Amish quilts were made with a plain weave wool challis, a forgiving fabric that can be steamed into shape. This is a soft, more drapable wool than the heavy wool used for coats and other heavy garments. It is particularly good for appliqué work. The colors were rich and, in keeping with Amish tradition, solid in color. No prints or woven patterns were used. Such quilts command high prices by collectors today. Wool is particularly good for appliqué work. Because many people shy away from using wool, we have included a section on working with wool (Chapter 2). We've also used an Amish quilt as inspiration for the project in Chapter 4.

YOUR TURN

We hope that our work will help all of you on your adventure into glitz. In the world of sewing, who knows what new materials and techniques will be invented? One thing is for sure: sewers and quilters will continue to create works of art. The equipment may change and new synthetic fabrics may be developed, but sewing is here to stay.

So throw out your fears, take a few risks, and choose something new to try. Start small and work up to larger projects. Most important, have fun and create something that gives you a sense of pride and accomplishment.

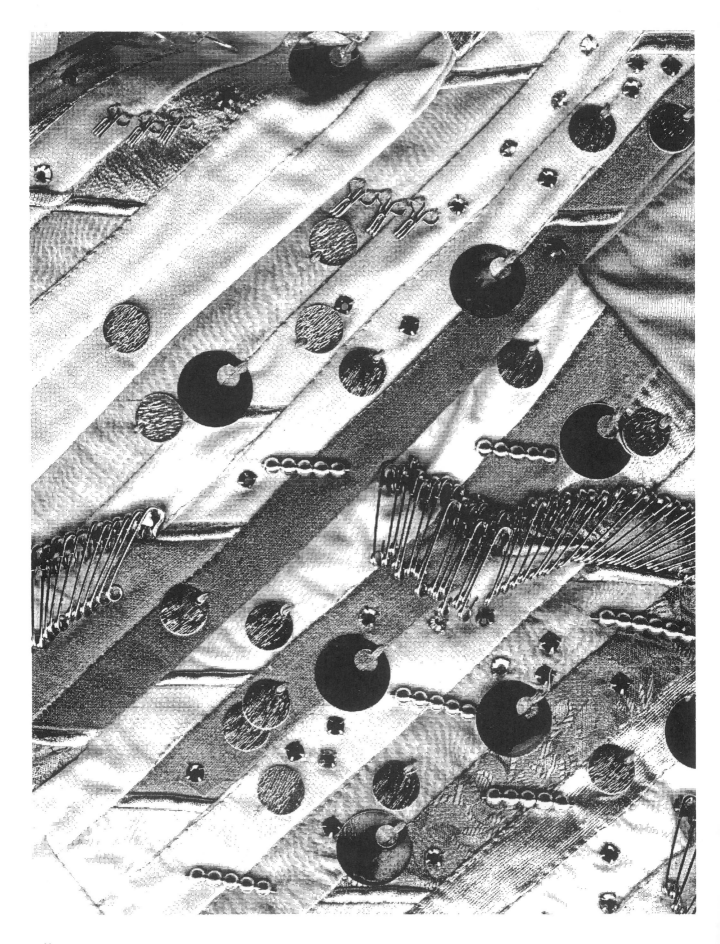

EQUIPMENT & SUPPLIES 1

GET READY!

Being prepared is the basis for getting your sewing projects off to a good start. Basic sewing includes care of your sewing machine, measuring, cutting, stitching (by hand or machine), and pressing. For successful results, the right tools are needed for each one of these tasks. Equip your sewing room with the tools you need to make your work easier and less time-consuming. Take good care of them, and they will serve you well for many years.

SEWING MACHINE CARE AND MAINTENANCE

It is most important to keep your sewing equipment in the best working order. Your sewing machine or serger will require maintenance—some by you and some by a professional. Both kinds of machines should be professionally maintained at least once a year by an authorized repair person. During the time between professional maintenances, your machine needs a consistent home maintenance routine.

After about eight cumulative hours of sewing, discard and replace the sewing machine needle. At this time, remove the bobbin and bobbin case (if applicable). You can buy a canned-air product from mail-order sources or at a sewing machine or camera store. Use this product to blow out all excess lint from the sewing machine. Don't blow into the machine, as your breath contains moisture, which will cause lint to collect in your machine. Blow out the lint from the tension mechanism; on the needle shaft above the removed needle; on the surface of the feed dogs; and around the removed bobbin case. Camera stores sell air brushes that work in the same manner. Use the soft brush that is part of your machine's attachment set to brush the lint off the top of the feed dogs and the underside of the needle plate. Replace the bobbin case and the bobbin, and insert a new sewing-machine needle. The size of the needle is determined by what kind of fabric and what size thread you are working with. We give size suggestions with each fabric used.

You should also clean your serger and blow it free of lint regularly. The needles do not need to be changed as often as sewing machine needles. The cutting blades should be sharp

and without burrs. If they become dull or damaged, replace them.

For both a serger and a sewing machine, use the best thread that you can afford. Inexpensive thread sheds a tremendous amount of excess lint, the enemy of all machinery—it acts as a sponge of sewing-machine oil. This results in drying out your machine parts, causing wear and tear.

Many new machines are permanently lubricated and should not be oiled. Wherever oiling is necessary, use only the sewing-machine oil recommended by your dealer for your machine. No other lubricant should be substituted. Be sure to wipe off all excess oil. A few minutes of sewing on scraps following oiling removes any excess oil before it meets up with your current project.

Take the time to familiarize yourself with your sewing machine. Take out your machine's manual and start reading on the first page. Read through the entire book, trying each technique as instructed. Experiment with each attachment and stitch to test your machine. Write notes in your manual's margins to help you in the future. If you know someone with a machine like yours, spend some time with her asking questions and exchanging ideas. Call your nearest dealer to see if classes are available on your sewing machine's use and care. Nothing is more frustrating than sitting down to sew and finding out that the machine is not working properly. Even worse is spending money on something you could have taken care of yourself had you been more confident and knowledgeable about your machine. Treat your machine like a trusted old friend, and it will reward you with faithful service for many years. (Chilton publishes two book series to help you, each brand-specific: the *Know Your Sewing Machine* series, by Jackie Dodson, and *Teach Yourself to Sew Better,* by Jan Saunders).

YOUR WORK SPACE

An efficient work space is an integral part of the sewing process. Many serious sewers are fortunate enough to have a separate sewing room or area used exclusively for this purpose. Others need to set up temporary sewing areas in a dining room, kitchen, basement, or other multifunction room when working on a project. If you must pack up your sewing at the end of every sewing session, it becomes almost impossible to accomplish much in the short time allowed for sewing because of the time involved in setting up and dismantling your machine and supplies.

No matter where you work, it is essential to have your sewing machine on a table or in a cabinet at a comfortable height. One way is to purchase an inexpensive, adjustable-height, armless office chair that can be set up to suit your body height in relation to the table's. These chairs swivel so that it is easy to get up and sit down. Most of these chairs are on rollers and will slide around easily, should your ironing station be close by, as it should be.

A comfortable height for sewing is most important. Your back is not made for hunching over machines for long stretches of time. You will soon develop neck pains and headaches from the strain. Remember, just because you might be fortunate enough to have your own sewing room with a special table, you still might not be working at a good height for your body. If you feel stress in your neck and back, check your chair's height and adjust it accordingly.

The sewing table should have both an area to the left of the machine and in back of the machine so that the fabric excess can lie on the surface around the machine and not drop to the floor during sewing. When this happens, the weight of the fabric pulls on the needle as you are sewing and causes the needle to bend or even to break. The pressure of this pulling on the needle can further damage the machine. It also causes irregular-sized stitches when sewing.

LIGHTING

Good lighting is essential to healthy eyes. Strain from too much, too little, or the wrong kind of light, can damage your eyes. Consider these ideas when planning the lights for your work space.

- It is helpful to have a floor lamp to light the sewing area, as well as an inexpensive clamp-on work light.

- The light should be directed at the sewing-machine needle area.

- If your work area is permanent, an overhead fluorescent light may be an efficient and good source of light.

- Fluorescent lighting can be bothersome to some people. You will have to test these out to see if they bother your eyes.

- Vita-Lites are fluorescent tubes which give off the same spectrum of light as sunlight. They are available at some health food stores or can be ordered at some hardware or lighting stores. These tubes provide a good source of light for choosing fabric colors with accuracy.

- Some fluorescent light fixtures may not be attractive in a home setting, but are fairly standard in an office space. If you want to spend more money, you could install more attractive wood-framed fluorescent lights.

- Sometimes indoor lighting can make fabric color selection inaccurate: a red inside the store looks different at home. During the day, move to a window or go outside for an accurate assessment of actual color hues.

- Good light is necessary in our cutting and ironing areas as well. Sewing in daylight causes less strain and renders color more realistic than sewing at

night, but when there is no choice, you can sew at any time—provided you have the proper lighting.

CUTTING TABLES

Most tables are 28" tall. Leaning over them can be uncomfortable on your legs and back, especially if you are tall. Fortunately, it is now possible to buy taller tables specifically designed as cutting tables. Ironing boards at full height measure about 35". This is a more comfortable height for most people. Some cutting tables are now manufactured at that height. There are large, table-sized cutting mats that can be placed on the table both for protection of the table's surface and to facilitate scissor and rotary cutting. The best tables are designed with a drop leaf so they can be effi-

Fig. 1-1: Create-A-Space table. When folded it measures 16" x 40", but it opens out to 72" x 40", which makes it ideal for sewers without a large work room. Photo courtesy of Bernina of America.

ciently tucked away when not in use (Fig. 1-1). Of course, you don't have to purchase one of these tables. An inexpensive alternative is a fold-away cardboard cutting surface called the Daynell table (see Fig. 1-2 and Source List). Our editor has used one in her small home for years and recommends it. Remember, the height should be comfortable for you. Convenience and comfort are the key words here.

IRONING AND PRESSING

The most efficient way to use an iron and ironing board is to set up the ironing equipment near the sewing area. Some quilters set up a small iron and tabletop ironing board next to the sewing area. Because quilters are generally sewing together lots of little pieces of fabric, and the seam allowances need to be pressed to one side as they are sewn, keeping the iron close is important. If you can sit in your chair at your sewing machine and simply turn your chair to use the iron, then you are working efficiently. Set your board up to the right height for comfortable ironing while you are seated. You will be both comfortable and efficient—the two things we strive for most when sewing for long periods of time.

Most quilters sew 1/4" seam allowances. These seams are not pressed open (in most cases) and are usually pressed to the darker fabric side. Careful planning of which direction to iron the seam is important when sewing pieces together where the seams butt. Try to get the seams to meet in opposite directions. This helps the seams join together perfectly. Garment sewers sew a 1/2" to a 5/8" seam allowance and the seams are usually pressed open. Since the garment sections are generally larger than patchwork pieces, the free-standing ironing board is better for the ironing process.

Fig. 1-2: Daynell fabric cutting table. Photo courtesy of Daynell Co., Inc.

Equipment

In some professional studios or workrooms the ironing area is a pad-covered board that is built like a tabletop and is stationary. These are available from tailor-supply sources or you can make your own by covering a board with a wool blanket and a sheet. Nancy's Notions (see Source List) sells a tabletop ironing pad, which can be folded for storage.

Household irons are now lighter and easier to handle than earlier models. Some even have automatic shutoffs. That is a good safety feature, but it can be annoying if the iron is left on during sewing time and you must use it every five minutes to keep it operating; however, it is easy to start up again because you only push a button. It doesn't take long to heat to the proper temperature. If you are forgetful, one of these automatic irons would be good for you.

The lightweight household irons do save some human energy. In the days when women spent long hours ironing their family's clothing, those heavy irons could be tiresome. Today, because of wrinkle-free fabrics, ironing is not as big a household chore. Heavier irons work better. Because of that, Black & Decker has brought back The Classic—their durable metal iron. It has a heavy-duty metal body and a polished aluminum soleplate with 25 steam vents. The extra weight and steam vents really make a difference, especially when you work with freezer-paper appliqué. Those nice crisp edges are so important for a professional appliqué look. Of course, this is a personal choice, but many sewers and quilters complain about the performance of their irons. The Classic iron is a good solution at a reasonable cost. Or, buy an old heavy iron from a thrift store. It won't have steam, but that can be simulated by misting the fabric with a spray bottle.

Some commercial and professional irons, retailing for upwards of $100, have a larger water reservoir and a higher capacity for steam than a household iron. They are lightweight and easy to handle. These irons are available by mail order, in some department stores, and in some sewing and quilt shops. If you don't see them displayed, ask the sales clerk if they are available. They help when pressing is important to shaping, especially in garment construction. In patchwork, some quilters recommend that steam never be used for ironing pieces because it can stretch them out of shape. This is true unless you are very careful. Practice ironing your patchwork and check your pieces with templates when you are finished. If your pieces are stretched, you are pressing too hard and pulling too much. Again, practice will help.

The ultimate iron for a serious home sewer is a professional high-steam iron. These irons retail for several hundred dollars. They are generally all-metal irons with a wooden or other non-heat-conducting handle. Some models are connected with a plastic tube to a bottle of water suspended from the ceiling. Purchased crystals sit at the bottom of the bottle to purify the water. Their disadvantage is that they are not easily moved from location to location because of the hanging bottle of water. Other models are connected with a tube and pump to a water source under the plate on which the iron can rest. This type of iron is a bit more portable.

All of these irons offer the ultimate service in ironing. They eliminate the problem of scorching fabrics. If you have one of these irons, you might want to keep another iron on hand for smaller ironing jobs, closer to your machine. If you are interested in purchasing a professional iron, check your local fabric shops to see if they could order one for you, or write to one of the businesses listed in our Source List.

If you have a sewing room and can leave your iron set up all the time, be sure it is unplugged when not in use. Set it back away from the edge of the ironing board or ironing surface, where it won't get knocked over by accident. Irons are tough, but falling onto hard surfaces from heights of more than two feet is not good for their plastic cases or for their interior parts. An airborne iron could also fall on a small child or pet, causing serious burns or other injuries.

Maintenance and Care

Your iron is more important to you than you realize. Take care of it so that it will be in good operating condition when you need it. If taken care of, your iron can last many, many years. First, learn how to clean your iron. Gunk may build up on the bottom surface, which will keep it from gliding across your fabric smoothly. Some irons have a Teflon surface, which helps keep foreign matter from sticking to it. The most common sticking problem is buildup from iron-on interfacings, fusibles, and other meltable materials. Commercial solutions are available for cleaning your iron's bottom plate. Clean & Glide and Iron-off from Dritz are two of the most common products of this type. Abrasive cleaners, such as SOS pads or Comet, will clean your iron, but will

scratch its surface and fill the steam holes with debris. You should read the instructions that come with your iron for recommended cleaning.

To help minimize the problems fusibles create, keep a few clean ironing board covers on hand. If you have worked with fusibles a great deal, you may have residue left on your ironing-board cover. Before starting a new project involving a great deal of ironing, be sure your cover is clean. If not, change it. If you will be doing a lot of fusing, you might want to use an old sheet or piece of muslin on your ironing board during the process. Remove the piece when fusing is finished and save for another project or throw away if too much residue has been left on it from the fusing process.

The type of water you use in your iron is important. If you use water directly from your tap (whether from a well or a city supply), it will contain chemicals or minerals that will build up inside and outside the holes on the surface of your iron. Well water is worse than city supply because of the minerals in the ground. The best water to use is distilled or rain water. If you can catch rain water and save it in a jug, a little lasts a long time. Most manufacturers do not recom-

mend leaving water in your iron for long periods of time. It could cause rusting and the rust could come out on your projects or clothing as you are ironing. Again, read your iron's instruction book to determine the best water to use and how to take care of your iron.

Ironing Press

Industrial presses have been in use for many years. Recently, smaller presses have been developed for home use. Most of the sewing machine manufacturers also sell presses.

The most common ironing press models heat only from the top half of the press. The bottom half is made with foam-covered wood with a fitted muslin cover. When the top is pulled down, almost 100 pounds of pressure is exerted on the bottom half. This pressure, combined with heat and steam, gives professional-looking results.

Although a press is not a necessary tool for the home sewer, it can save time in some ironing steps. Ironing fabrics after prewashing is easier with a press. Another good use for a press is for fusing interfacing to the back of fabric yardage—the even heat and pressure speed up the process.

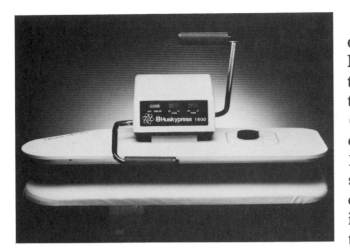

Fig. 1-3: *Huskypress 1600 Steam Master. Photo courtesy of VWS, Inc.*

The art to using the press is in arranging the fabric properly before lowering the head. Practice and experiment to perfect. Some hints for using a press are:

- Before pressing, smooth the garment or piece on the board.

- Allow approximately three minutes for heating time.

- Get in the habit of laying your fabric carefully on the pressing board without raising your hands too quickly, in order to avoid touching the heating plate.

- Leave the machine closed on your fabric or garment for a few seconds.

- After pressing, let the press cool down before closing.

- Read your instruction manual for more uses for your press.

Each brand of press has different built-in features. The Huskypress 1600 Steam Master, for example, has an electronic safety device built in. (Fig. 1-3). If the machine is operated and closed for about 10 seconds, a warning signal sounds. The electric heating is cut off. It is also possible to increase the opening between the heating and steam boards by a special button release. It has six heat settings. The handles have a safety feature to keep them from accidentally coming apart when not in use. These same handles make it safe and easy to carry.

An advantage that all presses have over the iron is that there is no movement or uneven pressure exerted during the ironing or pressing process. Also, there is no cord to worry about, and because the press is heavy and stable, it will not fall over easily. It does require more table space, as it has to be placed on a sturdy, flat surface.

Moistening Aids

Press cloths are useful to add moisture and prevent shine. Also, some of the stabilizers used by sewers and quilters are applied while using a press cloth. You can purchase a press cloth specially made for this purpose, or you can use a substitute from your own supply of materials. Some purchased press cloths are made of camel's hair, cotton, or wool. Depending on its use, hair fibers are found in varying percentages in these press cloths. But you don't need to purchase one. You can use what you have on hand. An old linen hand towel works well. Try those linen calendars you've collected over the years. They make wonderful press cloths—first be sure they are colorfast though. You could use a piece of scrap or leftover fabric from your project as a self press cloth. If it is important to be able to see through your press cloth while using it, cheese cloth or a transparent press cloth would be a good choice. A press cloth should be able to absorb and hold water. It will create and pass steam to the material beneath it when the iron is held on it. It will retain moisture for several pressings before you will need to add water to it again. In sewing rooms not close to a water supply, a small bowl or pail of water should be kept close by to keep your press cloth wet.

Another good thing to keep near your ironing station is a spray bottle filled with water. When a bit more moisture than the iron gives off is needed, you simply spray your project with the fine mist created by the spray. A clean, window-cleaner container works perfectly for this purpose.

Some fabrics must be pressed with a damp cloth, while others require even more moisture. Other fabrics cannot have direct contact with the heat of an iron. We will give hints for ironing specific fabrics as we go.

Special Pressing Aids

- A **tailor's ham** or pressing mitt is used for pressing shapes with curves such as a collar, dart, or sleeve cap. To retain steam, the ham is covered on one side with cotton and on the other side with wool. The mitt is used for smaller, hard-to-reach places and can be used over the hand or on a sleeve board.

- A **sleeve board** is a smaller version of an ironing board with two ironing surfaces attached together. It is used for pressing narrow areas like a pant leg or sleeve.

- Use a **seam roll** when the seam of your project might imprint into the under layer during the pressing. Usually only a small part of the project's surface is touched by the iron when a seam roll is used.

- A **point presser** or clapper is used for pressing seams in points and corners.

- A **velvet board** maintains the nap of velvets. It is rectangular and is covered with metal pin-like shapes that stick up from its surface. It looks similar to a metal dog brush, except it is larger. It is not a necessary tool, even for use with velvets, as a heavy terry cloth towel or another piece of velvet might serve the same purpose. But if you will be working with velvets frequently, you might want to have one of these helpful pressing tools.

CUTTING SUPPLIES

As a general rule, use the best products you can afford.

Rotary Cutter

The easiest method for cutting out strips of fabric is to use a rotary cutter. It is used for cutting other shapes and patterns as well. Rotary cutters speed cutting time and use less energy on the part of the cutter. If cutting with shears hurts your hands, then a rotary cutter can help. These cutters can only be used on top of a specially designed cutting mat with a self-healing surface which allows the cutter to cut on it without leaving ridges that will interfere when cutting is done again.

Cutting mats are manufactured in many sizes. Some are as small as 6" square, while others are as large as a whole table. The smaller mats are good for use when you are attending a class and need to carry many supplies along with you. Larger mats are best left stationary on a flat surface. If you stand them up on their sides, they tend to warp and may not lie flat when needed. The larger mats are made to roll and will relax and lie flat even after being rolled up for long periods of time. (*Caution*: Never set your hot iron on the cutting mat. It will irreparably warp.)

Some of the larger mats have measured horizontal and vertical lines printed on them. These lines are helpful guides when you need to know measurements quickly. They also help you check whether your fabric is placed perpendicular to your cutting tool. The lines are helpful, but not necessary for cutting.

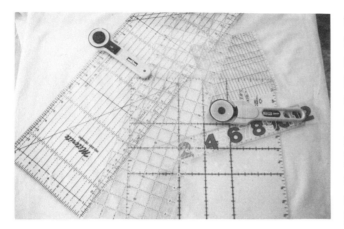

Fig. 1-4: Many types of Plexiglas rulers are available for measuring and cutting.

For fast, accurate cutting, lay out the pattern and fabric on top of a table-sized cutting surface. Place metal pattern weights or other clean, small, heavy, metal objects on top of the pattern pieces to secure the fabric and pieces in place. Then cut out the pattern using a rotary cutter, rather than shears. An alternative to using weights when cutting is to use a nonstaining fabric adhesive spray which is sprayed on the back of the paper pattern to hold it in place. Pins may be used; but if time is important, try the weights or the adhesive spray.

Guides and Templates

Many guides are available for measuring and for edges to follow during the cutting process. All shapes and sizes of Plexiglas measuring bars can be placed onto the fabric (Fig. 1-4). But if you constantly cut strips of the same width, consider buying metal strips cut to the widths you use most frequently. Metal templates commercially available start at 1/2" wide and go up to 3" to 4" wide. You cannot see through these strips, but they do eliminate the need to watch measurement lines on a Plexiglas bar. It is easy to use the wrong line on a see-through ruler if you don't mark it with masking tape before you cut. Those lines are hard to differentiate when you have only 1/4" to 1/2" separating them. Some of the metal strips come with a sandpaper surface underneath to keep them from slipping on your fabric while cutting. These strips would not be good to use on delicate fabrics which might get picks and pulls from the roughness of the strips.

Serger

An unthreaded serger may be used for cutting fabric strips as well. This is a fast and efficient way to cut fabric strips if many strips of the same width are needed. Mark the cutting line by laying tape on the fabric and cutting next to it with the serger.

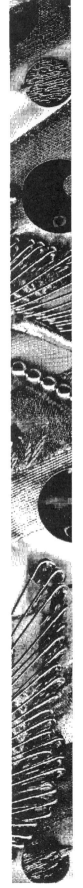

*Fig. 1-5:
Shears and
scissors.*

Shears and Scissors

Good, sharp scissors and shears are mandatory (Fig. 1-5). Scissors are not bent and have two handle holes that are the same size. Shears have a smaller hole for thumb placement and have bent handles to allow them to slide easily while cutting along a flat surface. Generally scissors are used for trimming small areas and cutting threads, while shears are used for large cutting jobs.

Fabric scissors and shears should be used exclusively for cutting fabric. They should not be used by family members for cutting paper or anything other than fabric, which will dull them quickly. When they become old and unsharpenable, they can be retired to paper cutting. Mark them with an identifying mark such as colored nail polish or by writing on an area near the screw with a dental pick or carpentry nail end. A good pair of paper-cutting scissors are a must for cutting templates out of cardboard and plastic. They, too, must be sharp and sturdy.

Beautiful scissors were found in the sewing baskets of days gone by. Attention to beauty in such a functional item was not uncommon. Beautiful scissors are available today as well, but remember that the function of the scissors or shears is to cut fabric with the least amount of resistance possible. If they can do that and be beautiful, too, all the better.

PINS

Good, sharp pins are necessary for sewing. Each type of pin should be kept in a separate pin holder.

- **Silk pins:** Used for light– to medium-weight fabrics. Available in several sizes: size #17 is 1-1/16" long; #20 is 1-1/4" long. Available with plastic or glass heads. Extra fine 1-3/4" are easy to see.

- **Ballpoint pins:** These pins have a blunt or rounded point and are used for knits.

- **Straight pins:** Metal headed pins generally used when a tissue pattern is used. Some straight pins have glass heads.

- **Longer, thinner straight pins:** These pins have plastic ball heads and are longer than the other straight pins. Some of these longer, thinner pins have flat floral-type heads. This makes them easy to grab. These are used mainly for pinning through several layers of fabric.

- **T-pins:** These are thicker pins with a T-shape metal head. Used for heavy fabrics such as those used in coats.

- **Pleating pins:** 1" long, used for pinning delicate fabrics in the seam allowance.

- **Quilting pins:** 1-1/4" long, used for going through more layers of fabric.

- **Safety pins:** 1" or #1 non-corrosive safety pins are best used to hold fabric layers together when machine quilting or pinning numerous appliqué motifs on a project.

Remember, pins should be noncorrosive and thin enough for use on appropriate fabrics. For example, a long, thin pin is necessary for pinning layers of patchwork with batting and backing. The pin has to go through many layers, but must not leave a large hole that will be seen when it is removed. If your pins are not rust-proof, they will leave stains in your projects if left pinned for long periods of time, especially during humid times of the year. If you have such pins, throw them out before you ruin any of your sewing projects.

NEEDLES

Your choice of sewing-machine or hand-sewing needles is important. If the proper needle is not used, the stitch quality is affected. Recommendations are given throughout this book for machine needle sizes to use with fabrics and threads. A good selection of all sizes and types of both hand- and machine-sewing needles is essential to perfecting your stitches.

Sewing Machine Needles

Many types of sewing machine needles are available today. The size of the needle to be used is determined by the fabrics and threads you are sewing and the type of stitch you are using. Your sewing machine manual makes good suggestions for this. As a general rule, a size #80/12 needle is used for everyday sewing. A #90/14 is used for heavier fabrics and threads. Remember, when you are machine quilting, the many layers require a larger needle (at least #90/14).

The chart below should help you with the size of needle needed for your project. European needle sizes are given in parentheses:

FABRIC TYPE	NEEDLE SIZE
LIGHTWEIGHT FABRICS: batiste, voile, crepe de chine, faille, satin, charmeuse	9/10 or 11/12 (65/70 or 75/80)
MEDIUM-WEIGHT FABRICS: poplin, pinwale corduroy, ottoman, gabardine, sailcloth, muslin, calicos, broadcloth	11/12 or 14 (75/80 or 90)
HEAVY-WEIGHT FABRICS: wide-wale corduroy, pant-weight denim, textured upholstery fabric, coatings, double-faced fabrics, canvas	14, 16, or 18 (90, 100, or 110)
KNITS	ball or universal point

Chart courtesy of Swiss-Metrosene, Inc.

Needles for Hand Sewing

For hand sewing, "sharps" are the needles most often used. The size is determined by the job you want to do. For hand-sewing tasks, such as sewing a binding down to the back of a quilt, you would use a #8 sharp. For quilting stitches, use a #8–10 or 12 "between" needle. There is no #11 needle, and the larger the number, the smaller the needle. Betweens are very short and thin with a rounded edge, and they help make the stitching easier. They take getting used to, as they are hard to hold at first. Once you learn to use them, you cannot use anything else. They help you to make tiny hand-quilting stitches.

Crewel needles are sharp and medium in length and are used for hand embroidery. Ballpoint needles are used on knits—sharp points pierce knit fibers while ballpoints push the fibers apart. Milliner's needles are long with rounded eyes; they are good for making basting or gathering stitches by hand.

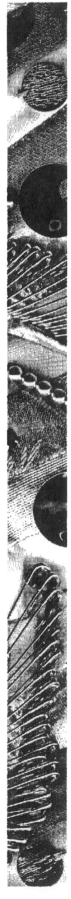

SPECIALTY NEEDS

For specialty sewing, many products are useful, but not necessary. **Thimbles** are useful for hand sewing. Many new versions are available that will fit any finger on your hand. These save wear and tear on fingers and help to make quilting stitches go all the way through all layers of the fabric. They are available in gold, silver, metal, plastic, leather, glass, and wood. Many sewers find it difficult to get accustomed to a thimble, but those who use them find they can't sew without them.

Bias bars, also called Celtic bars, are tools that help you make narrow bias strips for stems and other areas in appliqué work. These metal bars come in several widths (see Source List). Refer to the bias section in Chapter 3 for more information on use.

Alternative tools are available for making bias tape or strips. These tools allow the fabric to pass through and as it comes out, it is pressed with an iron (see page 115). The extra fabric is then turned under on each edge of the bias strip. These bias tape makers are manufactured in several popular sizes.

Other important but oft-forgotten tools are **presser feet** for your sewing machine. When you purchased your machine, you got several with it. However, many more are available for purchase through your dealer or by mail-order. When working with special fabrics and embellishments, some of these feet make the process much easier for you.

We mention many such feet in different sections of this book. A partial list includes: braid foot, darning or circular embroidery foot, roller foot, edge foot, cording or bulky overlock foot, zipper foot, open-toed foot, even-feed or walking foot, and plastic appliqué foot.

If you want to try some new techniques with your sewing machine, investigate the feet available for your own sewing machine. Sewing machines have either high-shank presser feet (approximately 1" between the foot turn screw and the feed dogs) or low-shank (approximately 1-1/2 " from turn

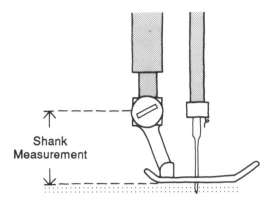

Shank
Measurement

Fig. 1-6: Presser foot showing shank.

screw to feed dogs). (See Fig. 1-6.) Some brands do not have every foot mentioned above available for purchase, and other feet will need to be substituted that will facilitate the stitching as necessary. New, generic feet are being developed to help solve that problem for the sewer who is frustrated with the foot selection available for her model machine. Watch mail-order sources and your local machine dealer for these new feet.

Every day, new tools are being introduced to help make the sewer's and quiltmaker's work easier. Many of these tools are useful and convenient, but not absolutely necessary to make a wonderful or creative project. Use your judgment and choose your equipment, tools, and supplies wisely. Remember that comfort should be your number-one concern. Convenience should come next, and if time is in short supply, your work space, machinery, tools, and supplies should all be the best you can afford, to allow you to work at your best. The goal here is to enjoy what you are doing and to be proud of all of your efforts as you display your finished project.

Threads are the hidden element in sewing. Too often we spend a lot on special fabric, but overlook the importance of using the proper thread. Because thread is such an integral part of any sewn piece and vitally important to the final results, it should be chosen with care. Making knowledgeable decisions concerning thread choices makes your creative work much easier. Look at your own local sewing supply store to see what is available to you. If you don't find enough choices, write to some of the addresses in our Source List for more information on their products. You will be amazed to see what information is available. Don't be afraid to try new threads. If they don't work for you, be persistent. Sometimes the threads really do add a dimension to your project that can't be added by any other medium.

If you haven't purchased threads in a long time, you may be totally confused by today's selection. You have many choices among the American-, European-, and Japanese-made threads (Fig. 1-7). As a general rule, purchase the best thread you can afford. Today, that price could be high, especially if you are using novelty threads. It can range from over $1 to $5 per spool. Your choice isn't always motivated by cost, but it does play an important role. We hope that this section on threads will help. Being prepared with the right threads will put you way ahead when it comes time to sew on the specialty items we cover.

The very worst thing you can do is to use old cotton threads on wooden spools that you've had around for years or that may have been your mother's or grandmother's. Despite their nostalgic charm, they should not be used for any sewing. These threads have deteriorated over time and they will not hold up in a sewn project. Save these threads to look at, not to use.

Fig. 1-7: A variety of threads from several manufacturers.

Cheap, bargain threads are also a poor choice. These threads are poorly manufactured, have imperfections, and cast off a lot of lint into the sewing machine when they are in use. They are not always colorfast and will run or bleed when moist.

Some purists feel that the type of thread used in the machine should match the type of fiber used in the fabric. For example, if you were sewing on cotton, you would use cotton thread. But fine Egyptian cotton thread sews other fabrics, including silks, equally well. Poly-cotton threads are the strongest of the regular sewing threads, but they can cut into fine natural fibers. Poly-cotton thread is, however, acceptable for sewing all types of projects if you are not an absolute purist. We want you to be aware that there are choices in sewing threads; you will develop your own preferences after testing the differences. We also realize that you may not have the instant availability of all thread types. Learn to choose the right threads from those that are available to you.

Some of the more common types of thread available are:

- Cotton-wrapped polyester— an all-purpose thread for hand and machine sewing on all types of fabrics, including natural fibers, synthetics, knits, and wovens.

- Extra-fine cotton-wrapped polyester—reduces puckering on lightweight fabrics.

- 100-percent mercerized cotton—used for natural woven fabrics such as cotton, wool, and linen. It has no stretch so is not suitable for use with knits.

- Long-fiber polyester—a smooth and even thread suitable for hand or machine stitching.

- Topstitching and buttonhole twist—used for decorative stitching, cording, and buttonholes, as well as topstitching.

- Hand quilting—a strong cotton or poly-cotton thread that has a coating to prevent tangling or knotting as it passes through layers of fabric.

Beyond these, there are many, many more types of threads available. We will attempt to cover the more useful ones in the following sections. No matter what thread you use, when sewing a large project, fill several extra bobbins. This will save time and interruptions during the sewing process.

Look for these important qualities when purchasing your thread.

1. It should be strong enough to do the intended job.

2. It needs to be the correct size and weight to give the right appearance and to be durable.

3. It should resist heat, shrinking, and abrasion.

4. It should also be colorfast—most important. *Note:* Several colors are difficult to make colorfast—red is the hardest one. Migrating colors will ruin your entire project, and they may not even have to get wet to run. Test a small piece of the thread before using if you suspect that there might be a problem with it.

How can you tell if a thread will meet these standards? It usually comes down to how much you pay. Better threads cost more.

The manufacture of threads is an interesting subject in and of itself. Although we will not go into the methods used for making thread, try to find out as much as possible about the types of thread you might be using.

MACHINE–QUILTING THREADS

The kinds of threads suitable for use in machine quilting are different from those for hand quilting. A waxy coating is added to help make the hand-quilting thread go through the fabrics easily. It is not intended to go through a sewing machine's guides. This waxy coating comes off and could be harmful to your machine.

Metrosene manufactures a machine-quilting thread that is designed for both machine and hand quilting. It is available in rare long-fiber 100 percent Egyptian cotton in thirty colors. The longer fibers help eliminate the snagging, knotting, and breaking caused by sewing through many thicknesses. It is not coated with wax so is not harmful to your machine. The highly used white and off-white colors are available in larger, more economical spools. If cotton quilting thread is not used, machine quilting can be done with regular poly-cotton, cotton, or rayon threads in both the bobbin and on the top of the

Butterfly jacket made from silk noil, tissue lamé, and an Alexander Henry butterfly print. A good example of three-dimensional appliqué. Machine-quilted in the ditch with silver metallic thread. Instructions for making a patchwork garment are given in Chapter 4. (Private collection, photo courtesy of Fairfield Processing Corp.)

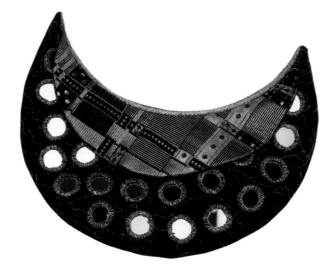

Evening bag by Walter Boyce. Uses shisha mirrors and woven ribbons and velvet. Ribbon from Offray, interfacing from J&R Interfacing.

This jacket was made with many types of fabrics, including men's silk ties, using a Folkwear pattern.

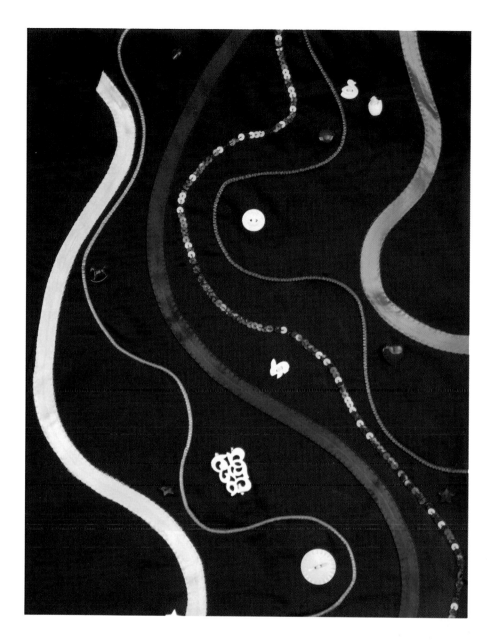

This McCall's pattern jacket uses sequin tape, sequins by-the-yard, rattail, satin bias tape, buttons, and machine embellishment (except for shank buttons). It is lined and unquilted.

Apron shows straight-stitch quilting. Cotton, Cotton Classic batting from Fairfield Processing Corp., gold metallic thread from Coats.

Ebb Tide *and detail 54" x 44", by Ruth Laine Bennett, Paoli, PA. Laces, cottons, lamés, three-dimensional appliqué, and many other embellishments. (Photo by Judy Smith-Kresley)*

sewing machine. With matching threads in the top and in the bobbin, no adjustment needs to be made on the sewing machine's tension. Machine quilting with these threads should be done with a #90/14 needle because of the thickness of the fabric and batting layers.

The thread that most resembles hand quilting is clear nylon or invisible thread. For the finest machine stitching use a very thin weight of the clear thread. It is wound on a thick cardboard core that serves as the center of the spool and is available in clear for white, off-white, and light fabrics, and in a smoke color for darker fabrics. In general, most sewers use clear thread on the top of the machine only. This thread does not work well in some bobbins. If you can use it in bobbin and top, you can prevent the thread from looping on the underside of the project (this problem is sometimes referred to as whiplash). Using a drinking straw on the thread spindle to hold the clear nylon thread spool also helps prevent this problem. You will need to test this on your own machine. The thread used in the bobbin is usually a color to match the backing of the project. It can be a thread of your choice, although many machine quilters recommend 100-percent cotton.

Balance the actual thread stitching so that the underneath stitches do not pull up into the front or top surface. You may have problems getting the upper clear thread to feed through the machine evenly. Sometimes the clear thread will snap off during stitching. If you haven't tried clear nylon, experiment with your machine and the following techniques or combination of techniques where applicable to your particular machine.

Try these easy techniques first:

- Lower stitch length to 0.

- Leave the clear thread on the spool pin and thread through the machine in the regular way.

- Lower the upper tension slightly.

- Lower the presser foot pressure.

- Feed the thread through the metallic thread guide between the spool pin and the tension wheel (if applicable on your machine model).

- Cover the invisible thread spool with thin plastic mesh, available in sewing stores or by mail order. Coats brand larger serger spools come with a covering inside the spool.

If that doesn't do the trick completely, try any of these:

- Fill the bobbin with clear thread. You may want to purchase a separate bobbin case for this purpose. Mark it with a dab of colored nail polish to differentiate it from your regular bobbin case. *Caution:* Some machines don't like clear nylon in their bobbin.

- Clean out the hook mechanism (if your machine has a removable one) with a soft cloth.

- Use a heavier, thicker nylon thread. This will be scratchy next to your skin on a wearable project, but it is fine for a project that either is non-wearable or will be used as wall art.

- Place the thread in a clean glass jar behind the machine. Feed thread through the machine as usual. The thread spool will wobble around the inside of the jar as you are sewing. Covering the thread in the jar with the same plastic mesh mentioned above also helps.

- Place jar on floor to the right of the machine. Tape a wooden or plastic spring clothespin onto the edge of the jar; feed thread through the enclosed ends. Tape another clothespin onto the right edge of the table; continue feeding thread through this and continue threading through the machine.

- If your machine has two choices of machine spool pin positions, try the spool on both positions before giving up.

If you are still trying to get it right:

- Purchase a separate thread stand. Place the thread stand to the right of the sewing machine. Feed clear thread through the top opening on the pole of the thread stand and continue through the regular threading of the machine; or place the thread stand more to the back right-hand side of the machine and tape a large hand-sewing needle onto the flat surface of the machine near the spool pin. The eye of the needle will stick out beyond the back side of the machine. Feed the thread through this hole between the thread stand and continue threading through the machine.

These suggestions may seem convoluted, but the end result of the quilting is worth the effort. This type of thread has heirloom-looking results; when used correctly, it resembles the time-consuming alternative—hand-quilting stitches. Remember one important thing about clear thread: It will melt when heated to high temperatures. Do not iron any machine quilting that has been stitched with this thread.

CHOOSING AND USING METALLIC THREADS

The wide variety of metallic threads now available allows the home sewer to glitz up her projects with a touch of glitter. Even if the background does not have glitzy or shiny fabrics, the threads alone can enhance the project. The metallic threads may bc used as the appliqué thread or as the background quilting thread. The glitter is not as noticeable until light hits the project in a certain way. The subtle addition of this little bit of glitz can make a plain project dressy. It looks particularly nice on solid-color cottons or tropical prints.

Metallic threads are available in a wide range of textures and colors. Purchase a spool of a variety of brands and types of these threads to experiment with. Be careful to read the description of the thread when ordering by mail. Be sure it is made for use in a sewing machine. Also ask the clerks in the fabric stores for help and information if you are unsure.

One thing that should be stressed when discussing the behavior of thread, metallic or otherwise, is that every sewing machine is different. Even if you and several of your friends have the same model machine, you may find your own machine reacts differently than theirs under the same circumstances. It is important that you be very familiar with your own machine.

With all metallic threads, first try a #80/12 needle to test the stitching. If the thread burrs behind the needle or breaks, change to a larger size needle—#90/14, #100/16, #110/18. If it still misbehaves, put the thread in the bobbin.

In general, if you can't sew a metallic thread through the top part of a sewing machine, you can use it in your sewing machine's bobbin case. However, we recommend that a second bobbin case be purchased for use with this and other unusual threads. This guarantees that your regular sewing bobbin's tension spring will not be damaged or altered while using these unusual threads. When these threads are used in the bobbin case, the projects are sewn wrong side up, rather than right side up, as in ordinary sewing. This lays the metallic thread on the surface.

Some thicker threads need to be hand wound onto the bobbin and the screw on the bobbin case's tension needs to be loosened. Test on scraps until you're pleased with the stitch. It takes practice and patience to match the thread to the tension on the bobbin case in relation to the machine's top tension. Sometimes you can't loosen a bobbin tension enough. Extremely heavy threads, such as 1/16" ribbon, novelty threads, pearl cotton, etc., must be threaded through the bobbin case opening. They should not be threaded through the tension spring; they override it. Don't worry; the thread will sew through the machine. If the threads will not sew in the bobbin case, they can be used on the upper looper on a serger for decorative serging.

When metallic threads are used for either decorative stitching or machine appliqué on an unbatted project, a piece of tear-off stabilizer should be used on the project. If the project has batting underneath it, it does not need a stabilizer. The batting acts as a stabilizer.

A project can be decorated and quilted using the top fabric and the underneath batting only. The batting will lie on top of the feed dogs. We recommend cotton or cotton-polyester battings for this type of work because they do not shift, they lie flat, and they don't get eaten up in the feed dogs. The quilted project is later lined to cover the batting.

The project can also be quilted or decoratively stitched through all the layers, including backing or lining. With decorative stitches, the stitch patterns may distort through too many thicknesses. You should test this on a sample first. We have been successful with metallic stitching through the single fabric layer top, Fairfield Cotton Classic (80-percent cotton/20-percent polyester) batting, and backing. Too much patchwork creates a thicker surface to sew decorative stitches through.

Fig. 1-8: Metallic thread dots showing through to back of quilt.

We recommend lowering the upper tension on your sewing machine slightly when using metallic thread on top. This should help make the stitches balanced on both the top and bottom. If the bobbin thread shows through to the top, or vice versa, you will need to adjust your tensions until they are balanced. Try testing your stitches on samples made from project leftovers until you have perfected your stitch. Solid colors are the hardest to sew on because the thread does not blend into the background print.

Ordinarily you would match your bobbin thread color to your top thread color. In the case of metallic thread on top, it is best to match the bobbin thread color to the color of the fabric on the back of your project. This will make it blend in better as you stitch. Sometimes, the metallic thread from the top will just barely show through to the back. The metallic threads will appear as colored thread dots (Fig. 1-8).

If they remain, even after you have worked at trying to balance the stitch or using a lighter-weight thread in the bobbin, you will have to decide if the effect created with the metallic thread on the top is worth this slight imperfection on the back. Since the strength of the stitch is not affected by this, it is a purely personal decision. It is also possible that the back thread will show through to the front, and this is not acceptable in the finished project. You will have to find a way to solve the problem or abandon the use of two colors of thread on the project. On a Bernina sewing machine only, feed the bobbin thread through the hole in the finger of the bobbin case to make the thread pull more toward the underneath stitching. Also, try a heavier weight thread in the bobbin.

Several companies offer metallic threads:

• Talon makes a metallic thread available in gold and silver. It is relatively thin and sews well with a #80/12 needle. This thread is good for all types of quilting and decorative stitching. When used for machine appliqué, the stitch length on the machine appliqué will need to be shortened to accommodate the thinner thread. Otherwise, there will not be good coverage over the raw edges.

- J. & P. Coats makes a metallic thread that is available in six colors. It has the appearance of a thicker, more textured thread, but it will sew nicely with a #80/12 needle with no breakage. The colors are muted and not as bright as other brands because of the texture and composition of the thread. On a thicker project, use a #90/14 needle to accommodate the thicknesses. Because it is thicker, Coats metallic thread will cover raw edges well in machine appliqué. The stitch length can be looser than those ordinarily used for machine appliqué.

- Sulky makes metallic thread in twenty-four colors. It is a thinner thread that is easily sewn with either a larger #90/14 or #100/16 needle. The colors are brilliant and have a high, smooth shine to them. The colors are very effective when used for decorative stitches. Sew at a slower speed and lower the top tension when stitching with this thread. When machine appliquéing, tighten the stitch length slightly.

- Gutermann makes many colors of metallic threads— the colors are more unusual. Some have overtones of two colors rather than one true color. These threads are textured and require a larger needle (#90/14 or #100/16).

The colors are not quite as shiny and clear because of the thicker texture, but the threads, when used for machine appliqué, can use a slightly looser stitch length. They can also be used for decorative stitching.

- One of the only metallic threads that was widely available to home sewers several years ago is made by Dritz. It is wound onto a long, plastic center cone, similar to that used for elastic thread. It is available in several colors. We were successful sewing with it using a #100/16 needle and stitching slowly. The upper tension should be lowered. It is slightly textured and it has a bright metallic sheen. Because it is slightly ravelly, it is a bit difficult to thread through a needle. (Newer model Pfaff and New Home machines have built-in needle threaders to help solve that problem.)

- Madeira makes a large range of metallic threads. This brand has a broader range of metallic threads for knitting, hand embroidery, serging, and sewing machines. They have a chart available (see Source List for address) that explains each of their threads' applicable uses. As an observant consumer, look on the bottom of any spool of Madeira thread and it will show you whether the thread in question should be used in a sewing machine; what size needle should be used; if it should be washed and ironed; and what other uses it has. Tiny symbols that may be understood universally indicate all of that information in a small space.

The smooth, thinner Madeira metallic thread is available in many colors, including variegated gold-color threads. These variegated threads can be very attractive for a different look in your stitching. These threads should be sewn with either a #90/14 or #100/16 needle.

The more textured Madeira metallic thread is a little trickier to sew. This metallic thread is available in more unusual colors such as light blue and chartreuse. It is especially nice for covering edges with decorative stitches. You should use a larger needle (#100/16) with this thread. We have had some problems with breakage on some sewing machines. We tried using larger needles and painting the actual thread on the spool with a clear fluid called Sewers Aid. This substance acts as a lubricant and facilitates the actual sewing. This product may be used on the bobbin thread, needle, and even on the bottom of the presser foot. Although it feels greasy to the touch, it does not leave a stain on fabrics or threads. It is available both in sewing stores and by mail order. (See notions companies in the Source List for address.) With persistence, we were able to get satisfactory results with this textured thread.

- DMC makes a thick, almost wire-like thread in gold and silver. It glistens like real gold and silver jewelry, but it is hard to sew. You need to use the largest needle (#110/18), and sew very slowly. This size needle is usually used for sewing heavy fabrics similar to denim jeans. The thread, being so wiry and thick, is spectacular in a project. Madeira also makes thicker gold and silver threads; they also require a larger needle. Try using it in the bobbin case or in decorative serging.

- A thin Japanese metallic thread, Kanagawa, is also available. It is a little difficult to sew with, even though it is thin. The metal thread fibers seem to twist when going through the machine's tension. You may want to experiment more with this thread, particularly on your own sewing machine. The advantage of this thread is that it is available in many shades of a wide range of colors. This makes it possible to match it to more fabric colors and to add shading to a machine-embroidery project.

When using metallic threads, you may want to experiment with them. Try using rayon thread, particularly 40-weight rayon thread, in the bobbin if other weights do not work. You may want to combine two metallic threads in the needle at one time; or combine a high-shine regular sewing thread, such as thin silk or rayon, combined with the metallic thread. You can also experiment with two threads running through twin needles on the machine.

With the large assortment of metallic threads available today, you can be more creative than ever with glitzy thread! When the desired results are achieved despite all obstacles, the aggravations of testing are worth the efforts expended.

CHOOSING AND USING RAYON AND RIBBON THREADS

Today's rayon threads are available in a wide range of colors from several manufacturers. Rayon thread, used decoratively, adds beautiful colors and sheens to a project. This little bit of glamour is not quite as obvious as the glitter of the metallic threads but is very effective. All of these rayon threads are very easy to sew. They can be sewn with a #80/12 needle. Rayon thread can be used on the top of the machine, as well as in the bobbin, if desired.

These companies also make variegated rayon threads that can be used to add interesting stitches in places where they will be seen. Machine quilting and decorative stitches sew well with rayon threads.

- Sulky makes rayon threads in 193 colors. They are wound on long, thin spools and there is a groove around the top edge that enables the thread end to be twisted back onto the groove for neat, easy storage.

- Madeira Mez-Alcazar (manufactured in Germany and distributed by Pfaff) and Coats also make rayon threads in a broad range of colors. Both of these rayon threads are wound on short spools.

- Two companies, Elna and Rhode Island Textile Company, supply a product called ribbon thread or ribbon floss. This is a soft rayon woven ribbon that is approximately 1/8" wide. It is wound onto a long spool and is available in both bright and soft colors, as well as in a few metallic sheen colors (Fig. 1-9). These ribbons can be used in the upper looper on the serger for decorative serging. They are applied to a project, rather than used to sew it together.

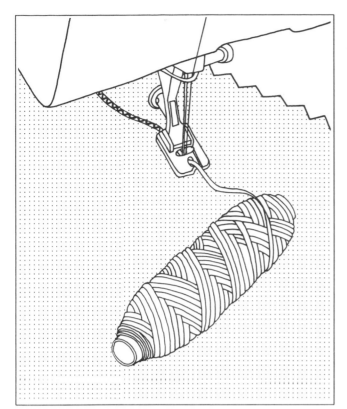

Fig. 1-9: Ribbon floss is being sewn on, using a braid foot to help direct the ribbon under the needle as it passes through the machine.

In combination with matching rayon threads threaded through the sewing machine, we wanted to topstitch ribbon floss onto a project. The textures and width of these ribbons were used to enhance the fabric, in combination with machine satin stitching on appliqué sections.

This ribbon thread is identical on both sides, so it can be folded back onto itself. The nature of the woven ribbon allows it to be curved, twisted, or straight stitched. The easiest method for stitching is to use a braid foot on the machine. This foot has an opening on the front of the foot that the ribbon can be fed into. This keeps the ribbon directly under the center position of the needle. Matching rayon thread

can be used for topstitching or zigzagging the ribbon in place. Bernina sewing machines have a knee-lift lever that raises the presser foot, making twisting and turning the ribbon while sewing much easier.

CHOOSING AND USING TOPSTITCHING THREADS

Many thread companies manufacture topstitching thread, generally in colors and sheens that match their own regular sewing threads. They are available in a limited color range.

When using topstitching threads decoratively, use a #90/14 or #100/16 needle to accommodate the thickness of the threads. You can purchase a topstitching needle designed specifically for this purpose. Regular thread is used in the bobbin case. These threads can be very effective when used either with a twin needle or parallel stitching, using the edge of the presser foot as a guide.

Topstitching thread is also used for outline embroidery. When stitching a heavy outline stitch (two stitches forward, one back, on newer sewing machines), it will resemble hand outline embroidery of the type frequently seen on the solid-color squares of Depression era quilts. Our method is an updated machine method. (See pages 30 to 31.)

Several brands of topstitching thread are available:

- One thread, Zwicky (manufactured in Switzerland and distributed by the Viking Sewing Machine Company), has a particularly high sheen to it. The regular sewing threads have a brilliance to them that is just short of the shine of rayon threads. They also make a topstitching weight thread in several colors.

- Gutermann makes variegated topstitching thread in two color sets. Although not shiny, this thread works particularly well with decorative stitches using a #100/16 needle. The cross-stitch motifs on some newer computer machines have the appearance of hand-stitched cross-stitch. Using a light ballpoint, long-eye needle might make topstitching easier with this thread.

- Zwicky also manufactures silk topstitching thread. As in their other threads, the colors are shiny and brilliant.

- Tire, a Japanese company, makes a silk topstitching thread that is heavier than Zwicky's. You need to use a #110/18 needle when topstitching with this thread.

- The vintage Belding Corticelli spool silk threads that are sometimes still available for purchase are not nearly as brilliant in color as Zwicky's colors.

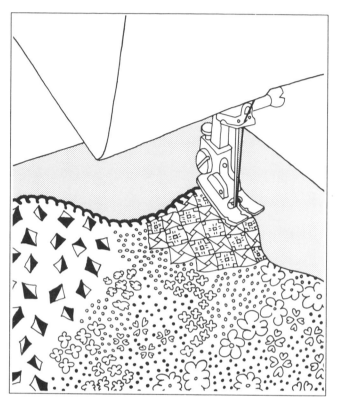

Another way to shine up a project is to use topstitching threads as a blanket stitch around an appliqué motif (Fig. 1-10). To accomplish this look, the edges of the appliqué motif need to be turned under. The sewing machine is set on a decorative blanket stitch mode or short blind-hem stitch and the appliqué piece is stitched in place. This is an updated machine method of earlier hand methods of appliqué and it is difficult to tell that the piece is not hand stitched; the results look the same. The topstitching thread should be in a contrasting color so that it will set off the

Fig. 1-10: Appliquéd piece being sewn down to a background using a contrasting color topstitching thread with a machine decorative blanket stitch.

appliqué. Imagine a silk appliquéd butterfly, decoratively stitched around with silk topstitching thread.

CHOOSING AND USING SILK THREADS

Silk threads, strong but thin, are available for machine stitching. Because silk thread is more expensive, use it in the top of the machine, with either rayon or regular thread in the bobbin case.

Janome, distributed by the New Home Sewing Machine Company, has several brilliant colors available. Belding Corticelli still manufactures silk thread. It is also distributed by YLI Corporation. (See Source List under Battings for address.) Tire, a Japanese company, also manufactures silk thread. It sews exactly like rayon thread and is distributed by Things Japanese. (See the Source List for mail-order addresses.)

Madeira now distributes silk embroidery thread, but it is unsuitable for machine sewing. The consumer information on the bottom of the spool states that it is suitable only for hand embroidery.

Gutermann now offers the full range of colors in silk. They are not as shiny as other silk thread and are used primarily in garment construction sewing, such as on silk or wool garments.

CHOOSING AND USING ELASTIC AND FUSIBLE THREADS

Elastic thread is used for sewing seams where stretch is important. Hand wind this thread onto your bobbin without stretching it, and sew either in seams or where needed on your project. It can be used to create a gathered look on fabrics to be used on garments or in quilts in creative ways. There are several brands available and some work better for particular functions than others. Usually a store will only carry one brand of elastic thread. You will probably have to order by mail to get a variety of threads to try. Place fabric in hoop, set machine stitch length to 0, and lower feed dogs. Free-motion stitch on fabric to cover the fabric surface. Allow for fabric shrinkage, about 3–6 times the fabric size.

Other thread products available for quilters are fusible threads. ThreadFuse and Coats Stitch 'n Fuse are two brands to look for. These threads are similar in weight to dental floss. They have a fusible coating that, when heated, will melt and fuse the sewn thread onto another surface. This type of thread should not be used in the top of the machine; it should be used in the bobbin only. When the thread is sewn underneath an appliqué edge and later ironed, the thread fuses the appliqué in place.

A good use for fusible thread is to sew it into seam allowances of thicker fabrics such as synthetic suede. The sewing line is about 1/8" from the cut edge of the seam allowance, parallel to the sewn seam lines. When the seam allowances are later pressed open and flat, the fusible thread will melt and adhere the under seam allowance to the background fabric. Other uses are for basting and positioning hems, zippers, trims, pockets, appliques, etc., before sewing in place.

Patchworkers use fusible thread to help them line up patchwork points and tricky joining seams. This product could be a real time saver for those stitchers who like to baste seams before sewing to make sure they fit properly.

ON TOP OF THE GLITZ: MACHINE QUILTING

There was a time when machine quilting was considered cheating. Many quilt competitions did not accept machine-quilted items for judging. Today, these same competitions are awarding prizes to machine-sewn and machine-quilted quilts. It is no longer considered a mistake or embarrassment to machine quilt. In fact, machine quilting has been recognized as a highly tuned skill and when done well, the results can be as breathtaking and spectacular as hand quilting. It is a timesaving quilting solution for today's busy sewer.

Many books on machine quilting are available, including *The Complete Book of Machine Quilting* by Robbie and Tony Fanning, *Heirloom Machine Quilting* by Harriet Hargrave, and *Fun and Fancy Machine Quiltmaking* by Lois Smith, which explain the machine quilting process well. We will explain the process only briefly. You have two general options: presser-foot quilting and free-motion quilting.

PRESSER–FOOT QUILTING

The first method of machine quilting is using the presser foot with the feed dogs up. This method, called "presser-foot quilting," is good for straight-line quilting because the presser bar lever does not need to be continually lifted. This type of quilting is the most difficult because the excess of the quilted project needs to be constantly turned through the opening of the machine between the presser foot and the right-hand motor/computer area. This can be cumbersome, especially with a large quilted project. Rolling up the excess in a long roll to the right of the needle is helpful in controlling the problem.

Set the machine on a longer stitch length, generally 3, or 8–10 stitches to the inch. Too tight a stitch length can cause puckering and fabric tucks, either underneath or on top of the project. The best presser foot to use is an even-feed or walking foot that will feed both the upper and lower layers through the machine evenly. An even-feed foot is available as an attachment for most sewing machines. Lessen the amount of pressure on the presser foot. Some newer machines are automatically self-

adjusting to pressure changes. Others need either a screw loosened on top of the machine or a dial turned to loosen the pressure. Newer model Pfaff sewing machines have a built-in even-feed foot in back of the presser foot. It snaps down into place when needed. It releases easily and is not in the way when not in use. In addition, it provides good visibility during the quilting process. This is an added convenience for the sewer who uses an even-feed foot often.

The newer Bernina sewing machines (those made after the model #930) are made with wider, better-quality feed dogs. They have a superior walking action and create a walking-foot action by themselves without the use of an even-feed foot. An even-feed foot can be used, but in many projects it is not necessary. You may want to test your own machine to see if this technique will work on it.

FREE-MOTION QUILTING

The second method of machine quilting is free-motion quilting (Fig. 1-11). This type of quilting requires practice, but it has more flexibility. It also makes quilting easier because the quilted project does not need to be turned around and around through the machine as with presser-foot quilting.

Fig. 1-11: Free-motion quilting using a circular embroidery foot.

With free-motion quilting, cover or lower the feed dogs on the sewing machine and set the stitch length to 0. A circular, darning, or embroidery foot needs to be attached. This leaves space between the foot and the feed dogs when the presser bar is lowered. The quilted project should be able to slide around easily under the lowered foot. If the plate that covers the feed dogs does not leave enough space when the presser foot is lowered, remove it. This will create enough space between the foot and the feed dogs. Even though the feed dogs are up, the free-motion movement can still be achieved. In Pfaff's Creative 1473 CD, the presser bar lifter needs to be set in a middle-down position to work correctly with the embroidery foot used for free-motion quilting. On a Viking 1100 lowering the pressure dial will create the necessary space for machine quilting. Get familiar with your own machine and practice before trying free-motion quilting. The machine doesn't sew properly if the presser foot is not lowered or adjustments are not set properly on the machine.

With free-motion quilting, your hands are what control both the stitching direction and the length of the stitches. The embroidery foot enables the sewer to guide the stitches around shapes and drawn lines, as well as make continuous fill-in stitches that are used to cover larger open areas. If you like the results of quilting around shapes in 1/4" increments (echo quilting), free-motion quilting makes this easy. If you prefer other types of quilting, experiment on samples before trying it on your project. Try free-motion quilting in shapes or in continuous lines resembling a jigsaw puzzle. If this method is done well, the quilting looks spectacular.

Jeanne Elliott, of Atkinson, N.H., teaches her students machine quilting with predrawn quilting exercises on paper. The student sews onto the paper patterns with an unthreaded sewing machine, preferably using previously used sewing machine needles.

Note: You can also quilt by machine-tying the garment or quilt. See Chapter 3, Buttons by Machine.

UNDER THE GLITZ

Sometimes it's what is underneath that counts. In the case of clothing, it is the interfacing that is underneath, and even though it doesn't show, it is an important part of a finished garment or sewn project. Interfacing is really a layer of material (woven, knit, or nonwoven) that is placed between the outside of a garment and its lining or facings. This layer adds shape, firmness, and stability. It should accomplish this without being seen or noticed. In patchwork clothing or quilts, interfacing is not as important for shaping, but because of the weight and composition of some fabrics used in these projects, interfacings are necessary for stability or firmness. In clothing, interfacings are most often used on collars, cuffs, lapels, waistbands, and other areas that require more body.

There are more than fifty brand names of interfacing from the four manufacturers we contacted, which makes choosing the right interfacing a confusing issue for sewers. We will not go into great depth to cover most of the brands because if you are making patchwork clothing or quilts, you will probably never need to use some of them. Still, it is good to have background knowledge from which to draw. If clothing construction is your interest, a tailoring book would be most helpful to you. To find useful books on that subject, try your local library or university, or consult our Bibliography.

INTERFACINGS

Interfacings are commonly available in three categories: woven, nonwoven, or knit. Woven interfacings are made just like fabrics and therefore have a grain. They will not stretch on the straight of grain, but do have some give on the crosswise grain. The bias has the most stretch. These woven interfacings are best used with woven fabrics. Nonwoven interfacings have no grain. Because they are not woven, they do not ravel. They are similar to felt in structure. Most nonwovens can be machine-washed and dried. Some nonwoven interfacings are made to stretch and are suitable for use with knits. Less common and more recently developed are the tricot-knit interfacings. Easy Knit, Fusi-Knit, Knit-Fuse, Quick Knit, and French Fuse are some of the brand names you might find in knit interfacings. They are all made with nylon tricot that allows a crosswise stretch while providing lengthwise stability. These products are used with knit or woven fabrics

Sawgrass Fire.
Folkwear pattern, Country Cotton fabrics from Concord House. Machine-quilted with silver metallic thread from Talon. Uses all types of lamés and many techniques.

Not Quite Amish, *59" x 59", 100% cotton solids from Springmaid, tissue lamé, Cotton Classic batting from Fairfield Processing Corp. Machine-pieced and machine-quilted with gold metallic thread from Coats. Detail at right.*

I Got Lucky, *a 36" x 36" wall quilt made with tricot-backed lamés and Concord House cottons. Machine-pieced and hand-quilted. (Photo courtesy of the House of White Birches. Photo by Rhonda Davis.)*

to give soft shaping with supple stability. Each of these products is fusible and lightweight.

For many years, Stacy was an innovator in the interfacing industry. Recently, they went out of business. The expected loss of products never materialized as other companies acquired the Stacy products. Along with this industry shake-up, new products have been developed. Pellon acquired several of Stacy's products and have left their names as they were. Therefore, several products still carry the Stacy name, while the Pellon name has been reserved for their nonwoven products for which they are so well known.

Another company to join the interfacing market through a blending of Stacy products is HTC or Handler Textile Corporation. In addition, Dritz, a sewing notion company, joined the apparel interfacing market when they acquired Stitch Witchery from Stacy along with a whole line of interfacings. Recently, Dritz acquired J&R Interfacing and now offers an extensive line of both sew-in and fusible interfacings.

Staple, another interfacing manufacturer, was not affected by the changes in the interfacing industry. Their products have remained stable.

There are two methods for applying interfacing—sewing and fusing. Sew-in interfacings are available in most fibers and can be woven or nonwoven. Generally, they are more durable than fusibles. Fusible interfacings are applied to a surface through heat. They can be woven or nonwoven with a resin on one side that bonds to the fabric when heat, moisture, and pressure are applied. After fusing, the surface of the fabric being fused will not feel as soft. Fusibles cannot be used on all fabrics because of the heat needed for the bonding process or the nap of the fabric. It is best to test a sample swatch before applying to your finished piece.

Choosing Interfacing

Choosing the right interfacing for the project can be confusing. Because there are so many choices available, the consumer has to do her homework before purchasing interfacing for her project. In addition, every shop or retail fabric store does not carry every product available. Mail-order sources are good, and many companies print a consumer information guide for their product. We have provided addresses of several of these mail-order companies in our Source List. Write to them to request information. Some companies may even send a

swatch sample card to show you what their products look and feel like.

You will find that we have recommended the use of several fusible products in this book. For instance, in the chapter on lamés, we recommend that tissue lamé be backed with a 100-percent cotton woven fusible interfacing to give it shape and to keep it from raveling when used in patchwork or appliqué.

Each company has a brand name for its product, and once you've become familiar with brands, you will remember their names. Learn to read the information on the end of the bolt when you are shopping for interfacing. When you are looking for a particular type of interfacing—100-percent cotton woven fusible, for example—look for that information on the bolt end. You will be amazed at what you will read. You will find 100-percent nylon tricot fusible; 100-percent polyester nonwoven fusible in several weights; 50-percent polyester, 50-percent rayon sew-in woven; and more. How do you know which one you want?

Start with your project. Why do you need interfacing? Is it for a collar or cuff? If so, you want a rather stiff material. What fabric will you be using for your project? Is it 100-percent cotton? Is the fabric a knit? If so, it will have stretching capabilities and so should your interfacing. Is your garment a tailored suit? If so, it might need a fusible weft-inserted interfacing to give it a crisp look. If it is a formal dress, sew-in woven interfacings might be necessary.

We tell you what interfacing to use with the fabrics covered in this book. However, there are some general rules for using interfacing that apply no matter what you are using them for:

1. **Choose a color that won't show through your fabric.** Most interfacings come in only two colors— white or black. Some are available in gray or bone. It is obvious that you choose white to use under a light color and black to use under a dark color. If you have mixed colors in your garment or project, as you

might in patchwork, or if your fabric is sheer, you need to experiment to see if the interfacing shows through on either color. If it does, decide which color value the fused fabric should be.

2. **Choose your interfacing based on the finished product and its use.** If you are making appliance covers, for example, you might want to choose Craf-T-Fleece. This is a sew-in needlepunched fleece made of 100-percent polyester. It adds warmth and loft to projects. It is great to use in pot holders, padded frames, crib bumper pads, and other projects where you might ordinarily use batting. It can be used with a wide range of fabrics. This product is available as a fusible, as well.

If you are making window shades or valances, you might want to consider a product called Create A Shade. This interfacing is a fusible nonwoven 100-percent polyester product that gives a crisp iron-on backing for home furnishings.

If you want to join two fabrics without stitching, you might need a product such as Magic Fuse. This is a fusible web-backed release paper which is 17" wide and is made of 100-percent clear polyamide. It is used for hems on skirts and pants and for appliqué in patchwork. This product is wonderful because the paper backing eliminates the old problem of such materials sticking to the iron when used. Wonder-Under is a similar product. These products have opened a new world for appliqué enthusiasts because they are so simple to use.

A new product available from Therm O Web is called Heat N Bond. It is most commonly used in the craft industry. It is a glue product with paper on one side. It can be used in regularly appliquéd projects, but it will also bond fabric onto wood or other surfaces. This would work well in home decorating projects.

3. **Preshrink your interfacing, even fusibles, before you use it,** particularly if the finished project is to be washed. Washing interfacing is not difficult but it is very important if it is recommended, since most interfacings will shrink. Quiltmakers are always told to prewash their fabrics. This is done for several reasons. One obvious reason is to preshrink the fabric. Another reason is to set the colors. Cotton will shrink and many times

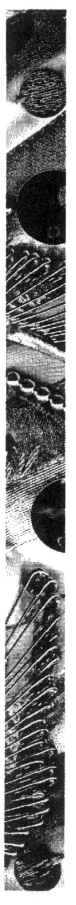

colors will run. If you are spending a great deal of time making a quilted garment or a quilt, you certainly wouldn't want it to shrink or have the colors bleed every time it is washed. If you have gone to all the trouble of preparing your outer fabrics, it is just as important to prepare the inside materials. Imagine that your outer garment did not shrink and your interfacings did. Your garment's shape would be permanently altered. Even if the project will never be washed, you must wet the press cloth to fuse the interfacing—and that can cause the fabric or interfacing to shrink.

To preshrink a fusible, simply place it in hot water and soak for 15 minutes or more.

Do not wring out water, but squeeze gently, and then place on a towel to soak out excess water. Open it up and leave it on a flat surface to dry. Placing a heavy towel over carpeting makes a good drying area. Remember that the fusing resin can be pulled off, so handle the interfacing gently. (You can also hang it over a shower rod.) Most sew-in interfacings can be washed in your washing machine and treated much the same way the garment will be when finished.

Common Interfacings Available

The chart on the next page lists four manufacturers and their products. The products compare with each other across the chart. For example, Staple's Jiffy Fuse compares with J & R's Fuse 'N Use.

INTERFACING CHART

J & R	STACY	STAPLE	PELLON	HTC	DRITZ
Fuse 'N Use		Jiffy Fuse		Stitch Witchery	Stitch Witchery
Quick Knit	Easy Knit	French Fuse	Knitshape	Fusi-Knit	Knit-Fuse
Stretch 'N Shape	Easy Shaper Lightweight	Jiffy Flex	EasyShaper	Fusi-Form	Shape-Up Lightweight
Classic Woven	Shape-Flex All Purpose	Shapewell		Form-Flex All Purpose	Shape-Maker All Purpose
Soft 'N Silky		Shape Up		So Sheer	
Tailor Fuse		Fusible Suitmaker		Armo Weft	Suitmaker
Magic Fuse		Transfer Fusing	Wonder-Under	Trans-Web	
Shirtbond		Fusible Shirt Maker	ShirTailor	Armo Shirt-Shaper	Shirt Maker
Craf-T-Back			Craftbond	Crafters' Choice	
Create A Shade			Decor Bond	Fuse-A-Shade	Shade Maker
Bridal Shape		Woven Durable Press		Veri-Shape Durable Press	
Woven Form		50/50 Durable Press		Sta-Form Durable Press	Sew-In Durapress
Craf-T-Fleece	Thermolam Plus	Poly-Fluff		Armo Fleece Plus	Big Fleece
Fusible Craf-T-Fleece				Fusible Fleece	Press-On Fleece

STABILIZERS

Tear-off stabilizers, although they aren't interfacings, do provide body and support to fabrics during the stitching process (Fig. 1-12). They are useful in appliquéing and for machine embroidery or decorative stitching. Their purpose is to add stability to the project during stitching, in addition to keeping finished stitches flat and neat. They can also be used underneath miniature patchwork piecing to aid in accurate seaming on tiny pieces.

You can also use water-soluble stabilizer for small projects, such as under shisha mirrors, buttons, or small appliqué shapes.

BATTINGS

Batting is another product that is not seen on the outside of your project, but is very important to what the outside looks like. Most of us associate batting with quilts. Generally its purpose is to add warmth and thickness to the finished project. The thickness, amount, or type of quilting desired determines what kind of batting should be used. There are other materials that can be used for insulation,

such as Thinsulate, but they are used mainly for commercial products such as sleeping bags and jackets. Because hand or machine quilting is generally considered a final touch on any patchwork project, the ease of stitching helps the quilter make the choice of battings.

What makes batting warm? First, it is the amount of air trapped in the fibers. Some fibers, such as down feathers, hold more air longer and are better insulators. Wool, silk, and cotton are other good insulators.

The thickness or loft of the batting is another warmth factor. The thicker the batting, especially natural fiber battings, the warmer the quilt or garment.

Fig. 1-12: Tear-off stabilizer being removed from the back side of machine appliqué.

Choosing Batting

Choosing a batting to use in your quilted project is not as easy as it used to be. Using what was on hand (whether it was pine needles, newspapers, or even horsehair in addition to cotton or wool batts), our quilting ancestors made beautiful quilts and some of those survive today. They are prized possessions of collectors. Today's quiltmaker, on the other hand, has choices. In order to make the right choice, the consumer needs to be made more aware of the products available.

Batting has traditionally been used as a filler to add warmth to a finished quilt or piece of clothing—therefore, the thicker the batting, the warmer the quilt. Of course, most of those thick quilts from the past were not quilted. It would have been much too difficult to hand-quilt through all the layers. Surviving examples of thick-batted quilts show that tying was the preferred method of holding the layers together. We can see how well that worked: sometimes all the batting is found in one area of the quilt because it migrated during use and washings.

Another purpose for batting in quilts was to show off quilting designs. Some of the finer antique quilts have the thinnest battings in them. The batting seems almost nonexistent, but you can tell it is there by the relief formed from the quilting.

We use battings for the same reasons today. However, we have many more choices and those choices can be confusing. To make the right choice in batting, you will first need to consider several things:

- Will you quilt by hand or machine? If you will be quilting by hand, you will need to consider the thickness or loft of the batt along with how easily a needle can pass through its layers. If you are quilting by machine, your choice is not as limited, because a machine needle will pass through a variety of thicknesses easily. Quilting stitches on cotton batt must be closer together than on a polyester batt, to prevent the batt from lumping. Remember, though, if you use 100-percent cotton on the quilt top, a polyester batt, and widely spaced quilting stitches, when you first wash the quilt, it will wrinkle badly.

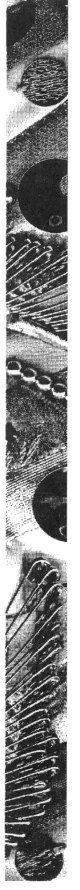

- What kind of fabrics will be used in the project? If you are using all cotton fabrics, you may prefer to use a cotton batting.

- What size will your finished quilt be? The batting chart at the end of this chapter shows the variety of sizes available in different brands.

- What is the end use of the quilt? If the quilted project will be used daily and will need frequent washing, a bonded polyester batt would be a better choice than a natural fiber batt.

- Some other qualities to look for in batting are drapability, resistance to fiber migration, loft, and softness.

Types of Batting
Natural Fibers—Cotton.
Quilted projects made with cotton battings drape naturally. In addition, cotton is easy to quilt and makes for a warm finished product because it has the capacity to absorb a great deal of moisture. This causes a cooling effect in the summer and makes it warm in the winter. One distinct advantage cotton battings have over the newer polyester battings is that they won't beard. Bearding is the migration of short batting fibers through the material to the outside layer. Bearding causes a fuzzy appearance on

your quilt top. It is especially noticeable on darker fabrics. There is a way to cut down on bearding which will be discussed in the section below on polyester batting.

Natural cotton fiber battings are still available today. Mountain Mist makes a 100-percent cotton batting of all bleached natural fibers, just as it did in 1846. This batting is a little less condensed than their Blue Ribbon Cotton Batting, which has an added Glazene finish to help hold the fibers together. This gives Blue Ribbon batting an even thickness all over. Without the finish, cotton has a tendency to pull apart when sandwiched between fabric layers before quilting. This creates areas of high and low loft (or thickness).

Quilted projects made with cotton batts should be quilted not less than 1/2" apart to hold the batting in position. Quilting stitches placed farther apart may result in bunching during the washing process and in use. Mountain Mist maintains that their cotton battings should not need to be prewashed.

Unbleached cotton battings are available. Warm Products, Inc., produces a product called Warm & Natural, which is a pure cotton, needle-layered batting. The pure cotton fibers are "punched" through a micro-thin polyester core. The core prevents tearing and adds strength. This product, available 90" wide, is guaranteed not to shift or migrate even if washed time and time again. It does not have to be prewashed. Even though it contains 10 ounces of cotton per running yard, it is only 1/8" thick. This batting feels almost like a blanket and does not pull apart easily. It does have small particles mixed in it. In processing, the average foreign matter content (primarily leaf and leaf-like particles) of cotton arriving at textile mills today is about three percent by weight. This may explain the small dark particles found in this cotton batt.

Wool Batting. Wool is another natural fiber that has long been used to add warmth to quilted projects. It is soft, drapable, and lightweight. Today's wool batts are needlepunched to prevent shifting, lumping, and fiber migration or bearding. It feels soft and is easy to handle.

Several companies are selling wool battings today and if you write to them, they will send you a small sample of their product to test and feel. Heartfelt, which manufactures 100-percent wool batting, guarantees its product can be stuffed, shoved, pushed, and pulled—it will do what you want it to do. Therefore, if you want a thinner batt, you simply have to stretch the batting from the center out. If you want a trapunto look, add batting to one place and take it away from another. Although we have not tested this on a project, the sample piece did stretch and stay in the stretched shape.

Wool batting is made from long virgin-wool fibers which are first scoured to remove dirt. Next they are moth-proofed, and finally carded or combed to open the fibers. Wool has a natural felting property which helps to hold the fibers together. It is not machine washable, but may be washed by hand in warm water and mild soap.

We found each of the three samples we tried to be soft and easy to handle and quilt. The thinnest of the three battings was the perfect thickness for use in clothing. It drapes well and provides a nice base to stitch to, even on the machine. However, the thicker battings can be made thinner by separating into layers, if the thickness as purchased is not satisfactory.

Of course, wool batts are much more expensive than cotton or polyester. For example, a batting 90" x 90" could cost as much as $45, compared with $7 to $10 for a batting of a similar size from other fibers. If you like using natural fibers, you will find wool a joy to work with, especially if you are quilting by hand.

Silk Batting. Strands of silk made by silkworms are used to make silk batting. These strands have not been spun or woven. The result is a soft and light white fluff which is formed into rounded cone shapes called "leaves." About 6 to 7 leaves are needed to make a long-sleeved jacket. About 30 to 35 leaves make one pound of batting.

Silk batting is lighter than down yet is extremely warm. Moisture will not affect the properties of silk fibers, so it is ideal for outerwear and special quilted projects.

Some modifications are needed when working with silk batting. Before working with the batting, cut out the pieces of the pattern to be quilted. Create a sandwich with the outer layer, thin interfacing of China silk, silk batting, another layer of China silk, and the backing. Encasing the batting in China silk prevents the batting strands from eventually migrating and bunching up. The batting has a tendency to stick to its adjacent silk fabric and stay where it belongs.

Working with the batting itself, you will notice that it is soft. Even so, the strands are very strong and, unlike cotton or polyester fibers, will break apart only with great difficulty. Don't try to pull the batting pieces apart. Cut with either a rotary cutter or sharp shears. Begin with one leaf at a time, slashing it up one side and stretching it out flat. Smooth and fluff up any inconsistencies or stiff spots in the batting as these will cause lumps as well as resistance to your needle. Now lay the leaves out on your partial sandwiches. Fluff the edges to blend the leaves together. Trim excess batting away. Add the remaining layers of the sandwich. Avoid excess handling of the batting. Secure layers with large basting stitches as for any quilting.

Keep your hands smooth when working with silk batting—any roughness will cause the batting to stick to you. Moistening your fingers as you work helps.

Little tufts of batting can work their way to the outer surface of your project. This can occur during the basting, quilting, or finishing process. Do not pull these tufts as they will only enlarge. Clip away the strands as close to the surface of the fabric as possible.

Your silk batted project may be washed in lukewarm water by hand or machine using a mild soap—not detergent. To hand wash, fill your tub with water before adding your project. Accordion-fold a quilt and place in the tub. Soak for 15 to 30 minutes. Drain and refill tub with cold water. Repeat rinsing process several times to remove all residue. Note that the quilt will become quite heavy when wet. This causes strain on the seams and quilting lines, so handle gently. After rinsing, blot the quilt with towels and roll up in an old mattress pad to absorb moisture. Lay quilt out on a flat surface and when almost dry, place it over several clothes-lines to dry completely. Depending on the outside fabric, some wool, cotton, and down battings can be treated in the same manner.

To machine wash your project, follow the same procedure for hand washing. Set machine on gentle cycle. You might want to eliminate the agitating process as it will put strain on the seams. Dry as explained for handwashing.

Despite the extra work required, using silk batting is worth the effort. It is luxurious and lightweight, making it a good choice for garment construction—especially when silk is used as the outer fabric.

Silk batting can be purchased by mail order (see Source List for addresses). It is more expensive than other natural fiber battings because it has to be imported.

Cotton Blend Batting. The Fairfield Processing Corporation produces a blended batting that combines the good qualities of cotton with the easy care qualities of polyester. Made of 80-percent cotton and 20-percent polyester, Poly-fil Cotton Classic is nonallergenic, hand washable, and easy to handle and needle, and it shows fine quilting details. Another advantage we have found to using Cotton Classic, especially when machine quilting, is that once it is sandwiched between the top and the backing, the batting helps keep the layers from shifting during the quilting process. This is an advantage

during machine quilting when the quilt is moved around a great deal under the head of the machine. Some other battings are much smoother and are hard to keep in place. Cotton Classic is not as easy to hand quilt as the 100-percent cotton or the polyester battings, but it is not impossible to get small, even stitches.

Although it is not necessary to prewash Cotton Classic battings, some quilters prefer to prewash anyway. To prewash, place in washer on gentle cycle in warm water. Forego the washing cycle and simply set your machine to the rinse cycle. After spinning, remove batting from machine and place in dryer to dry. This will prevent any shrinking after quilting when the quilted project is washed.

Polyester Batting. Polyester was the answer to the home sewer's prayers. It provided ease in handling, care, warmth, and strength. Fabrics could be washed and worn without ironing and colors did not fade. Batting manufacturers chose to use polyester in batting for the same reasons. This new product changed the quilting world forever.

The traditionalists among us point out that polyester is a plastic—a petroleum by-product.

They argue that it deteriorates, beards, and could even deposit oil blotches on quilts. It could burst into flames and will melt when burned. Not only that, but polyester batts are coated with plastic resins to prevent lumping and shifting. Sometimes these resins make it difficult to quilt through.

Of course, all of those comments are truthful, but polyester battings have really added a new dimension for quilters.

Polyester fiber brands that are familiar to us are Dacron, Kodel, Fortrel, and Trevira. Because polyester is a resilient fiber, a project made with polyester batting will hold up to the abuse of washing and use. It is lightweight, non-allergenic, and cannot be harmed by mildew or moths.

According to Donna Wilder, Director of Marketing at Fairfield Processing, polyester batting is produced by feeding polyester fibers into a carding machine where they are combed into parallel rows or layers and laid into a blanket form by a machine called a cross lapper. The loft and weight of the batting will vary with the number of layers used in the blanket. Additional processes may be necessary to produce the wide variety of polyester battings available today.

As the blanket comes off the machine, it is called unbonded batting. The weight and thickness varies, with 3 " being about the thickest loft available commercially. If the batting is unbonded, it has a loose construction. This makes the batting difficult to work with and creates areas of high and low loft. Without a finish the fibers tend to migrate or beard through the fabric to the top layer of your quilted item. Even with the bonded finish, bearding can still be a problem. We have found that when working with dark fabrics, especially black, the bearding really shows. The small fibers seem to work their way to the surface and stick there.

Bearding may be eliminated by covering an unbonded batting with cheesecloth or a lightweight fabric. Of course, this adds another layer to quilt through—possibly two layers if these materials are added to both sides of the batting—thus making it harder for hand quilters to make small, even stitches.

Bonded battings are given a light resin coating or glaze on both sides. This coating adds strength and helps to lock the fibers in place. A newer heat-sealed process creates a similar

effect. Bonded battings usually have a higher loft. The bonding process makes it possible for less quilting on projects to hold the layers together.

Hobbs Bonded Fibers has created their Poly-down DK especially for quilters using dark fabrics in their quilting projects. This batting is dark gray in color and even though fibers still migrate (even in resin-treated, bonded battings), the dark fibers will not be as noticeable with dark fabrics as with the traditional white battings.

Needlepunched Batting. Needlepunching is accomplished by passing the blanket of fibers through a needling machine called a fiber locker. This machine has a number of barbed needles or hooks mounted on a grid which vibrates up and down. As the blanket passes through, the needles pierce it and entangle the fibers as they withdraw. Nonwoven blankets are made using this same process. The loft of the finished batting is determined by the number of layers in the original blanket. This batting accentuates fine details of quilting and is used in quilted clothing.

All of these batting choices for quilters today can be confusing. The wide variety of types and sizes available makes the choice difficult. Because we have experienced the disappointment of the wrong batting choice in a finished item, we know how important it is to choose the proper batting in the first place. Most of the batting companies have consumer sample leaflets available and would be happy to mail you one. Use the samples to find your preferences. (Refer to our Source List for addresses.) If you are still unsure, purchase the smallest size batting available in the type you'd like to try, and use it on a small project—something you can put together quickly. The wrong choice in batting can ruin the finished results of something you have worked long and hard to create. Because batting choice is so personal, our recommendations would not be beneficial to you. Even between the two of us, our preferences differ. They differ from project to project as well. Becoming an informed batting consumer takes considerable time and energy, but is worth every minute in the end.

Recommendations by Loft

For warmth in quilting: A dense, low-loft cotton or needlepunched polyester batting 1/4" to 1/2" thick.

For tied quilts: A high-loft bonded or unbonded polyester batting 1" to 3" thick.

For fine hand quilting and clothing: A low-loft, less dense polyester, cotton, or cotton-blend batting.

For beginning hand quilting and machine quilting: A medium-loft bonded or needlepunched polyester batting 1/2" to 3/4" thick.

The chart on the next page shows some of the brands available, their fiber content, sizes available, and a brief description of the product. At the very least, this chart will show you just how many choices you have. Some of the companies have batting available by the yard in different widths. Hobbs has the most selection in this area with several choices and widths available.

Take advantage of the consumer education materials available from each company and make your batting choices with a higher degree of knowledge and confidence to make your heirloom quilted items last for generations to come.

BATTING CHART

BRAND NAME	FIBER CONTENT	SIZES AVAILABLE	QUALITIES
Poly-fil Traditional [1]	100% polyester needlepunched	36 x 45", 45 x 60", 72 x 90", 90 x 108", 120 x 120"	Handles like a blanket, shows fine quilting
Poly-fil Ultra-Loft [1]	100% polyester needlepunched	45 x 60", 72 x 90", 81 x 96", 90 x 108"	Extra thick for warmth. Hard to hand quilt
Poly-fil Low-Loft [1]	100% polyester	45 x 60", 81 x 96", 90 x 108", 120 x 120"	Bonded, tiny stitches possible
Poly-fil Extra-Loft [1]	100% polyester	All sizes except 36 x 45"	Used for comforters, bonded
Cloud Lite [2]	100% polyester	All sizes except 36 x 45" and by the yard	Resin-bonded, low loft
Cloud Loft [2]	100% polyester	45 x 60", 81 x 96", 90 x 108", 120 x 120"	Hi-loft, resin bonded
Poly-Down [2]	100% slick hollow-core polyester	Same as immediately above	Easy quilting, less bearding
Poly-Down DK [2]	Same as Poly-down	90 x 108"	Gray color for dark fabrics
Thermore [2]	100% polyester	27 x 45", 54 x 45", 45" roll	Thin, no bearding, for clothing
Heirloom [2]	100% polyester needlepunched	45" wide by the yard	Good for unusual sizes
Resin-bonded polyester [2]	100% polyester	48" to 96" wide by the yard	Available in thick and thin lofts
Mountain Mist [3]	100% polyester	All sizes including 36 x 45"	Soft, good for first project
Quilt-Light [3]	100% polyester	45 x 60", 81 x 96", 90 x 108"	Small stitches, thin batting
Fatt Batt [3]	100% polyester	72 x 90", 81 x 96", 45 x 60", 90 x 108"	Extra thick, Glazene finish
Mountain Mist Cotton [3]	100% cotton	81 x 96", 81 x 108"	Bleached, Glazene finish
Blue Ribbon Cotton [3]	100% cotton	90 x 108"	Can quilt 2" apart, lightweight
Cotton Classic [1]	80% cotton, 20% polyester	81 x 96"	Blended to resist bearding
Warm & Natural [4]	100% cotton	90 x 90"	Unbleached, specks visible
Heartfelt [5]	100% wool	60 x 90", 80 x 90", 90 x 90", 90 x 108"	Needlepunched, soft, 1/2" thick
Taos Mountain Designer Light [6]	100% wool	36 x 84", 72 x 94", 80 x 90", 90 x 94", 94 x 108"	Needlepunched, thin, drapes
Taos Mountain Traditional [6]	100% wool	Same as immediately above	Can be tied in 8 – 10" intervals

1. Fairfield Processing Corporation
2. Hobbs Bonded Fibers
3. Stearns Technical Textiles Co. (Mountain Mist)
4. Warm Products, Inc.
5. Heartfelt
6. Taos Mountain Wool Works

CHOICES

2

Before you begin to sew, you usually have a purpose, a plan for what you want to produce—anything from a simple skirt or wall hanging to a complicated garment or quilt. For some people, the planning stages are easy. They pick up a magazine or book, find a pattern they like, and buy it. The pattern instructions tell exactly what and how much to buy and show step by step how to complete the project. Many home sewers or quilters never change anything on a pattern because they like it just the way it is.

Other sewers work with purchased patterns as guides, but the finished project in no way resembles the one shown with the pattern. These sewers are willing to take a few risks, even if they are not sure exactly what they want their finished item to be—as they go along, they formulate their ideas. Sometimes they change things many times before they get it just as they want it. Along with this creativity comes a real satisfaction when the project is complete.

We'd like to help you make the leap from the first kind of sewer to the second, in this chapter. We will pose some questions to you to help you make some of your decisions. Let's begin with garment construction and go on to quilts or other nonwearable quilted items.

CHOOSING A PROJECT

Whether you make clothes or quilts, you need to consider some general questions before you start. The first is the time factor. When do you need it? Is this a project you want to work on at your leisure, enjoying every minute, or do you need it tomorrow? Of course, the more time you have, the more details you can add and the more experimental sewing you can do.

In the end, if you have chosen to take your time on this project, will it be worth your efforts? Will this project be used or will you get discouraged and never finish it because you took on too much at once? Only you can answer these questions. You have to know yourself and how much you want to risk when you start on something new.

Unless you have unlimited funds available to support your sewing, you will have to consider the cost of your project. Most garments require a pattern, interfacing, lining, surface fabrics, embellishments, and notions. Quilts, too, require many yards of fabric. All of that adds up. You could spend over $100 per yard for some exquisite fabrics. That isn't practical unless you are sure your skills are up to sewing on such material. If you are a real risk taker and you can afford the risk, it might be worth a try—if you really love the fabric. A quarter yard of a $100 per yard fabric seems like a bargain at $25.

An alternative to making your own project from scratch is to buy a plain ready-made garment or to use one of your completed quilts and embellish it. Think about ways it could be glitzed up without tearing it apart. Could something be applied on the surface to give it some sparkle? Could an accent piece make some changes? Deciding whether to alter a completed piece can be fun. The decision doesn't have to be final. You can make up different ideas into samples and attach them to the garment or quilt with pins and look at it for a while. If you like it, you could opt for a more permanent attachment and then sew it on. If you don't like it, you can

remove it and try something else. A denim jacket is a good example of a garment that can be appliquéd and decorated. (See Fig. 2-1.)

CLOTHING CHOICES

If you want to make a one-of-a-kind garment, you must first choose what type of garment you want. This decision should be based on many things. One of the most important considerations is your sewing skill. Are you an experienced sewer? Are you familiar with your machine and ready to try new things? If you feel that your sewing skills are adequate but need challenging, then you are ready to take the plunge and try something new and unique.

The second consideration in choosing your project is wearability. Do you want to wear this item daily, weekly, or only once? If you are wearing it daily, do you want it to attract attention? From experience, we know that some pieces are so smashing that other people cannot help commenting on them. That makes for good conversation no matter where you are, but if you are shy, you may not like it. Therefore, consider where you want to wear the item, and how much attention you want to attract.

Once you have made up your mind about the wearability of a garment, you are ready to choose the project. Perhaps you want an accessory. A wonderful place to start is a flashy belt. It can be heavily embellished, and when you are wearing it, it may or may not be noticed, depending on what else you are wearing with it. If you wear it under a jacket to shop, no one will see it, but if you wear it to a meeting with the right clothing, everyone will notice.

How about a border on a skirt, vest, or jacket? If the embellishments are simple, they will fit in almost anywhere on a garment. Of course, remember practicality. You wouldn't want to add sequins to your everyday skirt. It wouldn't wear well and couldn't be laundered.

It would be a good idea to work the pattern up in muslin first to see if you like the fit enough to risk it in a more expensive fabric. This muslin trial pattern should be saved for future use if you think you might want to make the same pattern again. Make your changes and notes right on the muslin and it will become a permanent pattern. Use it to cut another muslin background piece on which you can sew your patchwork. See Chapter 4 for more information on these sewing steps.

You may want to be extravagant and make a garment to be worn only a few times or at a special occasion—such as a wedding. This one garment will be your masterpiece; perhaps you will want to embellish the entire surface of your garment. In this case, consider several things. Comfort, for example—a garment could be the most beautiful ever made and not be wearable because it is uncomfortable. It could be too heavy if it is covered with too many buttons, sequins, and beads. It could be too warm if there are too many layers of patchwork and batting. It could be too stiff if embellishments have been overdone. Most of us want to be comfortable after spending so many hours on a garment. But some people don't care. Their whimsical attitude is, "If it is worn only occasionally, and for a special event, who cares how much you have to suffer?" Ann's garments made for the Fairfield Fashion Show are all the mandatory size 10 and Ann will definitely never get into any of them; yet the satisfaction she feels in her finished work more than offsets the fact that she won't ever wear the garment. She considers these pieces as art that she has created.

Could you buy what you want already made? If so, how much more or less expensive would it be than what you will end up spending on your own creative version? It's no longer

true that you can sew it yourself for less than you could buy it. Ready-made garments are often inexpensive (especially if they were manufactured in foreign countries), and when you compare the cost of similar fabrics, you could buy the item ready-made for less. Are you sure you want to spend the time and money on something that can be purchased for less at your local shop?

Of course, when you buy ready-made, so do others. Yours won't be any different. If it is one-of-kind you want, you must make it yourself. The satisfaction you get in the end does not have a price tag attached. Pride in accomplishment cannot be measured in dollars and cents.

QUILT DESIGN CHOICES

If you are not a clothes horse and have no desire to embellish and play with fabrics on clothing, perhaps you would like to make a one-of-a-kind quilt. Some considerations are needed here as well.

The use of the quilt is the number one consideration. If the quilt is to be used on a bed, it cannot be covered with beads and sequins. People sit on beds; they throw other items of clothing on beds; they sleep in them and cover themselves up with the quilts; their animals sleep on them. Can you imagine covering up with a quilt that makes noise when you move it around? It could snag in your hair or you could even swallow something from it and choke to death in your sleep. This is extreme, but the point is to know the final use of the quilt.

Most art quilts are hung on the wall. They are displayed in places where people will see

Fig. 2-1: Appliquéd denim jacket shows how a purchased garment can be dressed up.

them and enjoy looking at them. This type of quilt can be embellished in imaginative ways. If this quilt is made for a particular room, perhaps it could be coordinated with other decorative items in the room. That color could be used as an accent, such as a lamé that does not overpower the quilt, but adds some excitement to the overall design. It will be noticed, yet it won't overpower the viewer as being there.

Rethink your reasons for making your projects before you begin them if you want to create one-of-kind or original designs. It is difficult to make a mock-up of a garment. You can make a sample that will help you with fitting problems, but you can't actually make a miniature jacket and know if it will work on you. A quilt, on the other hand, can be tested in miniature by drawing up the design and pasting small patches in place to see how the colors and the design work together. It will not be an exact replica of the completed item, but it will help you make some decisions long before you have started the construction process.

You will see some outrageous garments and quilts at various judged events and shows around the country. Most of them were made to attract attention or to test a skill. Most of them were not made to be used—ever. Your creativity should be combined with practicality, unless you are an artist who just wants to indulge yourself in your own whims. Therefore, think about your project a long time before you invest your time, energy, and money into it.

PATTERN SELECTION

CLOTHING PATTERNS

Many brands of patterns are available to the home sewer today (Fig. 2-2). Of course we are all familiar with *Simplicity, McCall's, Vogue,* and *Butterick.* But there are others.

European pattern companies include *Burda, Style, New Look,* and *Nue Mode.* Burda patterns require marking and adding a seam allowance when cutting. European patterns sometimes offer a more unusual selection of styles than American companies. The European fashion industry is the forerunner of all the new, hot fashion trends. American designers attend fashion shows in Paris and other European cities each season to get insight into the fashion trends far before they appear in this country. The European patterns sometimes reflect this influence.

Kwik Sew and *Stretch & Sew* patterns, available at some fabric stores, are created for

Fig. 2-2: Many pattern companies compete for the home sewing market.

sewers who are looking for more extensive pattern selection both in garments and in unusual items such as lingerie, bathing suits, and ski wear. Kwik Sew patterns use a 1/4" seam allowance just like quilters use. Most other commercial patterns use a 5/8" seam allowance.

Folkwear patterns have been reinstated through the owners of *Threads Magazine*. These patterns have the look of clothing from bygone days. They have an ethnic look and often use lots of fabric. They are sewn with a 1/2" seam allowance. Other ethnic patterns are available by mail order (see Source List).

Patchwork Clothing Patterns

In the quilting business, many patterns have been designed especially for patchwork and embellishment by small companies and designers who market their own patterns. (See our Source List.) They have been designed for special fitting problems related to the added bulk of patchwork seams and batting layers. Even though commercial pattern prices have risen rapidly over the last several years, these small entrepreneurs are competitively priced.

If you have decided to make a patchwork garment, it is best to use a pattern with few darts and fitted seams. Ready-made patterns can be adapted for patchwork and appliqué with a few changes.

Adaptations for Patchwork Accents

In order to incorporate patchwork as an accent onto a pattern, the easiest method is to choose a pattern that has a separate section that can be used as an accent section. This can be a large collar on a blouse or dress, or a yoke section on a shirt dress. If you want to add a patchwork section on part of an existing pattern section, the pattern piece can be cut apart. When this is done, you need to add a 1/2" or 5/8" seam allowance onto each cut edge. You can do this in several ways. You could eyeball the additional 1/2" or 5/8" or maybe you would prefer to write directly on your pattern to guide you. You can also cut up old pattern tissues and tape a seam allowance to each side of the cut pattern.

On a collarless jacket, dress, or blouse, add the patchwork to the facing pieces and turn them outward to the top side instead of to the inside. This is an interesting and easy concept in adding patchwork to a pattern.

Adaptations for Totally Patchworked Garments

On a garment that will be totally covered in patchwork, it is best to make the patchwork in sections; in other words, you will create patchwork yardage from which you will cut your pattern pieces. After the patchwork is completed, pin the pattern onto the patchwork and cut it out. If this patchwork is to be batted and quilted before constructing the garment, add 1" extra seam allowance around the entire garment. Batt it and machine or hand quilt it. Then place the pattern piece on it again and recut it to the exact size. When pieces are batted and quilted, they tend to change and shrink in size. This technique is a safety net for correct sizing.

If you choose to quilt three layers together (top, batting, lining), you will need to finish seam edges, either with seam tape or serged edges. However, the quilting can be done without the lining fabric underneath. It is easier and neater to free-line the garment after the patchwork and quilting are complete. After unlined seam allowances are sewn together on the sewing machine, the excess batting is carefully snipped out of the seam allowances. The seam allowances can then be either pressed open and flat or serged. Serging untrimmed batting in

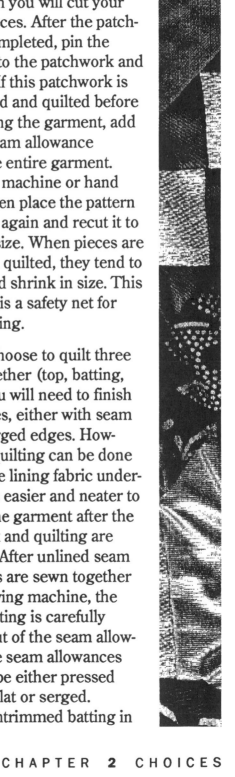

the seam allowance, particularly with patchwork seams, is too bulky and thick and is not easy to serge accurately.

Adaptations for Appliqué

Appliquéing the garment is easy if the appliqué is to be limited to one pattern section. When positioning the appliqué shape on this section, remember to leave room for seam allowances outside the appliqué section. If you appliqué over two sections, seam the two sections first, press seam allowances open, and appliqué the motifs over the seam allowances. This will work for curved and fitted seams, as well as darts.

Adaptations for Beading and Hand Decoration

If you plan any beading or hand decoration on the finished surface, do it before the garment is lined. Be sure to consider seam allowances and leave room for the presser foot to sew the seam allowances together. Remember that you can't easily iron the garment, so choose a nonwrinkly fabric for the foundation.

To be creative in your sewing, you need to look at patterns differently. Try to imagine what they might look like with your creative additions or embellishments. Try to work more freely with patterns, adapting them to your preferences. You may want to make sketches first. Remember to keep a record of your changes, in the event you might want to use the pattern again in the future on another project.

An easy way to experiment is to use waxed paper and a tracing wheel. Lay a light spongy fabric like wool flat on a table. Place your pattern on it and waxed paper over that. (If the waxed paper isn't wide enough, fuse two pieces together with a dry iron. It won't hurt the iron.) Trace the pattern outlines with the tracing wheel. Then try new design lines on the waxed paper. If you don't like the results, crumple the waxed paper and start again. Your original pattern is still intact.

Remember when making a garment that the embellishments you add should be flattering to you and your figure. Making a smashing jacket that wins a prize in a fashion show is wonderful, but if you can't wear it because it is too small or doesn't fit you right, then you won't have the satisfaction of wearing it with the same pride.

*Fig. 2-3:
Samples of
vintage
quilting
patterns
available for
the quilter of
the past.*

QUILT PATTERNS

Fortunately, today we have many sources for quilt patterns. In the early days of quilting, women didn't have the myriad of choices of magazines or books to choose from when trying to decide on a quilt pattern (Fig. 2-3). Many syndicated columns written in the 1930s shared a quilt pattern each week or more often. Some magazines and books have revived those patterns and are sharing them with their readers. (See our Bibliography.)

During the last few years, many new quilting magazines have been added to the already extensive list of quilting publications available. Quilters seem to have an insatiable need for magazines to satisfy their quilting urges. Most of these magazines share patterns in each issue.

In addition to magazines and books, quilt pattern companies are thriving as well. Visit your local quilt shop and you will find patterns for whole quilts in all sizes (Fig. 2-4). Some companies sell quilt kits through craft catalogs. Patterns and ideas are everywhere. (See our Source List.)

Some quilters decide on a pattern and copy it just as it is in the instructions, using the exact same fabrics and colors as shown. Others see a design and use it as a starting place to make a quilt that barely resembles the original.

If you are adding embellishments and glitz to your quilts, they will be unique even if you do use commercial patterns or those designed by others. Regardless of where the original idea came from, when you finish with it, it will be far removed from the original, if you let those creative ideas come through.

What are you waiting for? Choose your pattern and begin deciding what fabrics and colors to use. Now you are ready to begin experimenting with glitz and before you know it, you will be shimmering on to your next project in style.

*Fig. 2-4:
Samples of
quilt patterns
available.*

FABRICS

HOW AND WHY WE BUY

The old question "Which comes first, the chicken or the egg?" applies to sewing and quilting as well. Is it best to choose the design first and then the fabric, or should it be done the other way around?

If you want to be economical, and use every fabric from your stash before buying more, you should be planning your projects and/or purchasing your patterns before you ever look at a piece of fabric. Determine how much fabric is needed. Give yourself a general idea of what you want; then put on your blinders, head for the nearest fabric store, and purchase just what is needed and no more. Of course, if you want to add or change something halfway through your project, it will mean another trip to the store. You cannot be spontaneously creative if you work in this fashion, but you won't waste any fabrics. If this is how you work, you're probably the kind of person who would only work on one project at a time, and you really finish them.

On the other hand, you may be the kind who purchases fabric on a whim. Do you spend a great deal of money on fabrics you might (probably won't ever) use? You're one of the compulsive fabric hoarders—they lurk everywhere. It is difficult to recognize them, but they tend to frequent both fabric stores and sewing and quilting conferences. They cannot resist the feel of the fabrics and of having them stockpiled in their closets, boxes, shelves, and other hiding places. These people have a passion for fabric. Whether sewn or not, it gives them great pleasure to own it. Like squirrels, some of these people are known to hide their fabrics, particularly away from the eyes of their family members and friends. We know of one fabric store in California that bags fabric purchases in brown grocery bags to disguise them as they are brought into homes. If you are one of these, get out your fabrics first, then choose a pattern and design.

Every fabric you buy must be considered in terms of wearability, care, cost, availability, and personal impulses. The needs of your projects are intertwined with the fabrics you choose. If you are making a jacket, for example, you must be concerned with warmth, wearability, and care. If you want to wear it every day and to wash it periodically, you must purchase your fabric accordingly.

Washability

Check out the fabric's washability before purchasing it. If it is a fabric you own already, test wash a scrap if it has not been prewashed. If it runs, you will have to prewash it to prevent further running in future washings. To do this, you will need to immerse the fabric in a full-strength solution of white vinegar. Do not mix the vinegar with water. Once completely wet, wring out and rinse in warm water several times to see if color still runs from the fabric. If so, do not use it—if not, dry and iron to prepare it for use.

If your fabric shrinks considerably, you should also prewash the remainder of the fabric before use. If the fabric simply breaks down, then you cannot wash it ever, therefore its use will be limited to unwashed projects.

Warmth

Some fabrics are warmer than others by nature of their fiber content—wool, for example, is a very warm fiber. Therefore, if you want to make a dressy jacket for summer wear, wool should not be included in its construction. A quilt might be made only for decorative qualities and not be needed for warmth. If this is the case, the batting to include should not have such warming qualities. A thick, polyester, high-loft batting is made for more warmth. Again, a wool batt would provide more warmth than a polyester one. But the wool batt would need special care; it should not be washed. It is also more expensive. Consider these things as you choose your batting (see page 43).

Wearability

Wearability is hard to test. Several fabrics discussed in this book do not wear well. It is obvious that lace should not be used on a pair of everyday pants. It just will not wear well. It is much too delicate for the abuse it would have to take. Common sense and knowing more about fabrics in general make the wearability choice easier.

Cost

Almost all home sewers are concerned about the cost of the fabric. Most of us sew to save money and to make our projects one-of-a-kind. There was a time when a great deal of money could be saved if clothing was home-sewn. In recent years, inexpensive factory labor has enabled purchased, ready-made clothes to be cheaper than home-sewn clothes. Even so, the pleasure and price of home sewing are the main reasons many people continue to sew.

Saving money means that you shop at sales, compare prices from shop to shop, and

make use of every scrap of fabric. In making patchwork projects, frugality is a virtue. After all, we all use scraps in our patchwork quilts and projects from time to time. Fabrics that sell for $30 to $70 per yard may seem extreme for most home sewers, while others would not hesitate to purchase the expensive fabric if it is what they need or want. If cost is a real factor, you should sit down with the list of materials needed to complete your project and see exactly how much it will cost. If it is more than you can afford, is there a way that you can cut down the cost? If you can find a less expensive source, it would help. Maybe you can make a trade with a friend who has what you need. Perhaps you can wait for a sale. Regardless of how you accomplish the price reduction, if it is an important project, you should not abandon it because of price. You might have to postpone it until you have gathered everything you need, but don't give it up entirely.

We hear a great deal about peer pressure when talking about adolescents. Adults experience peer pressure, too. If you are at a fabric store with a friend, she will almost always try to talk you into purchasing something if she is. She doesn't want to feel alone in her purchase. She might talk you into buying something you never would buy otherwise. Her urging you to try something new, or telling you how great that color would look on you encourages you to buy something you might never use. If you have this problem, you might be better off to shop alone. Of course, this could backfire because it might give you more time to spend in the store, allowing you to purchase more. If this is the case, you might benefit from leaving your checkbook and credit cards at home and taking only a small amount of cash with you to the shop.

Impulse buying is an important consideration, especially if you are in a fabric store that you may never visit again. It's almost as if you need to purchase fabric just in case they stop making it. We have found this fact to be true, especially in specialty fabric stores. It is true that similar fabrics are in the same chain stores, but small "Mom and Pop" stores actively seek out the unusual to stay in business. This type of purchase is not wrong, but it should be controlled, depending on your personal financial situation.

Finding Supplies

Availability of supplies is a big factor for some sewers. They may live in isolated areas where fabric stores are few and far between. If that is your case, you need to become more familiar with mail-order sources (see our Source List). Almost everything you need can be purchased through the mail. It may cost more because of the postage, but you might save money in the long run. First, you won't do any impulse buying because there is no temptation right at your fingertips. Second, you won't have to drive from shop to shop in your car, which could save money if you're the kind who makes special trips to the fabric store just to buy one spool of thread. If you do shop through the mail, you must be very sure of your needs because you cannot slip out and buy more right away. Most mail-order fabric companies have swatch cards and/or literature to help you make your choices. You do not have to abandon the project due to lack of available supplies, unless you are in an extreme hurry for the items. If all else fails, there is always next-day delivery.

WOOL

Wool has been used in Amish quilts for many years. When the Old Order Amish settled in Pennsylvania, they had strict doctrines regarding clothing colors. They could use only black, navy, blue, gray, purple, and brown in their clothing and their homes. They were prohibited from wearing printed or patterned clothing. The colors used in their clothing provide the basis of their textile arts. Their palette still is composed of the earthy, natural colors that comprise their world— pastel colors are not part of it.

The solid-colored wool challis that was available to the early Amish is hard to find in the same Amish colors now. Rayon challis or a combination of wool and rayon challis in many prints are more readily available, and blends are easier to launder and care for than 100-percent wool challis. Many of the 100-percent wools in shops today are in heavier weights and have many colors in the weaves.

It is possible to mail order a large range of solid-color wools, in a heavier weight than challis, but in a lighter-weight wool than used for outerwear clothing. This type of wool is available from the Dorr Mill Store. (See Sources List for the address.) A wide range of color choices is available that makes these lightweight wools an attractive choice for both patchwork and appliqué. Of course, these wools can also be used to make wonderful braided and hooked rugs.

Many wool fabrics are also available in fabric stores. Be careful to check the fiber content of these wools on the bolt end. Generally, 100-percent wool is more expensive than blends. Because of the

color choices and different weaves available, wool mixes well in patchwork. If you are a purist about fiber content, you may be limited in shopping for colors and textures within the 100-percent wool fabrics available. Artistically, you might have to be willing to sacrifice fiber content in order to achieve a good fabric mix.

Wool is made 54" to 60" wide and, therefore, you will need less yardage than with other fabrics for your sewing project. It can easily be cut with a rotary cutter or shears for patchwork projects.

Wool presents few problems in sewing. It usually is thicker than cotton or other fabrics used in patchwork. This thickness has a tendency to feed unevenly under a regular presser foot, but an even-feed foot will keep the two layers sewn perfectly flat and even. Wool does not ravel much, so no particular care needs to be taken on the seam allowances, although many tailors trim the seam edges with pinking shears to keep the seams neat.

Because of the heavier weight of the fabric, seam allowances on wool projects may be more bulky than other fabrics. To reduce bulk, try sewing seams with a serger. A serger will cut down on seam allowance bulk and the pieces will evenly feed through the machine, as they do when you use an even-feed foot on a regular sewing machine.

Wool presses extremely well; it is the most forgiving of all fabrics. Tailors use it for men's suits because it conforms and shapes to body curves when pressed with a damp press cloth and a good steam iron. Special pressing tools, such as a tailor's ham, help with shaping. Because of this pliability, wool fabrics are wonderful for appliqué by hand or by machine. The shapes will lie flat after appliqué without puckering. Because wool has tiny fibers sticking off its surface, it sticks to itself and other fabrics fairly well. This is an advantage in appliqué, because the wool doesn't shift around much during the stitching process. It is not always necessary to use a fusible to hold the shapes in place during sewing.

Creative use of wool in patchwork is endless. Several well-known patchwork clothing makers and quiltmakers, such as Jo Diggs, Cheri Raymond, and Diane Herbort, work extensively with wool. Landscape designs can be duplicated from nature with the wonderful weaves and textures of wool. Trees and grass have real texture that cannot be duplicated with other fabrics. Yet patchworkers have almost ignored the inherent capabilities of wool in their work, probably due to the cost and care factor involved with wool. But if you are not concerned about laundering the finished piece, wool deserves a second chance from you in both quilts and quilted clothing.

Although there are currently some washable wools, wool and wool blends should generally be dry cleaned. This could be a disadvantage if wool is combined in garments or quilts with other washable fabrics. Still by careful shopping for wool and wool blends, you may uncover enough washable wool fabrics for a washable project.

Another disadvantage to using wool is that it is susceptible to moths. Moths can permanently damage a wool item. When not in use, it is best to store your fine woolens in cedar closets or chests or with anti-moth chemicals.

SILK

Originating in the Orient, silk is a natural animal fiber that has been used for centuries both as fabric and as thread. Consumers like it because it is beautiful, warm, and lightweight. It has an excellent affinity for dyes and is absorbent but dries rapidly.

Silk making begins with two varieties of silkworm: wild and cultivated. The fibers of the wild silkworm are yellowish brown, and have a coarse, hard texture. This worm feeds on scrub oak. The cultivated silkworm requires sanitary and quiet surroundings. It feeds on mulberry leaves and produces finer, yellow to gray fibers.

A silkworm lives about two months, during which time it passes through four stages of development: egg, worm, cocoon, and moth. In the worm stage, it eats about 30,000 times its initial weight and sheds its skin four times. When spinning its cocoon, two filaments are ejected from the mouth; one an almost invisible silk filament, and the other a glutinous substance which hardens when exposed to the air. In about three days, the worm covers itself with these filaments. In order to obtain the fibers, silk workers do not allow the moth to emerge from the cocoon. The cocoon is heated with hot air or steam to kill the larvae, and then the thin fibers—as long as 1350 to 4000 feet—are reeled from the cocoon and manufactured into silk threads. It takes approximately 2500 to 3000 cocoons to make one yard of silk fabric. It is no wonder that silk is such an expensive fabric.

Noil silk is made from the waste created from spun-silk manufacturing. It does not have the sheen and luster of reeled silk.

Next to nylon, silk is the strongest fiber among fibers of the same diameter; comparable to good-quality iron wire in strength. Not as strong when wet, silk has elastic qualities that allow it to stretch before it breaks.

Although silk care information on commercial garments states that the silk should be dry cleaned, a home sewer can, in most cases, prewash silk before it is sewn. This can make a home-sewn garment more economical than a ready-made garment that must be dry cleaned. Silks can also be painted, marbleized, and dyed at home. This can be done on both China silks (thin) and silk noil (thick). Creating your own fabric colors can truly individualize your sewing.

China silks are about one-third less expensive than silk charmeuse, but are about twice the price of calicos and cottons. They are very wiggly and slippery to sew. If you use these silks in patchwork, cut, pin, and sew them with care. Sometimes covering your cutting surface with a large piece of flannel or felt will help to hold the silk flat while you cut. This would work for pattern cutting with shears rather than for using a rotary cutter. Silk charmeuse—shiny and vibrant—is particularly wiggly. Great care must be taken to keep it straight while

cutting strips and pieces with a rotary cutter.

If these types of silk are incorporated with other types of fabrics, it is best to fuse them with a lightweight interfacing to stabilize them. This works nicely, but you need to test a small square of both the interfacing and the silk to see that the interfacing adheres properly.

When pinning silk, use thin silk pins in the seam allowance. The pins should be new and without burrs. Silk is very sensitive, and the holes left by pins and needles can show in the finished project, so take care when pinning and sewing. If a seam needs to be removed, the holes left by the needle and the stress from the ripping process will show on the fabric.

If only thin silks are being sewn together on the sewing machine, you should be using a #70/10 needle. When mixing up fused silks with other fabrics, a larger, #80/12, sewing machine needle should be used.

If these silks are to be used for machine appliqué, you should fuse them first with woven cotton interfacing to stabilize them. After the fused interfacing and silk have cooled off, fuse the underneath interfacing again with a second layer of paper-backed fusible webbing. The shapes can be

This beautiful ball gown, **Midsummer's Night Dream**, *was designed by Ann Boyce for one of the Fairfield Fashion Shows. It uses Polished Apple from Concord House, tissue lamé, ribbon silk, and hand-beaded embellishments. Machine-quilted with Talon metallic thread. (Photo courtesy of Fairfield Processing Corp.)*

Close-up of ball gown shows bias lamé and three-dimensional flowers. (Photo courtesy of Fairfield Processing Corp.)

Silk tissue lamé, satin, corduroy, silk, and velvets are combined on this jacket (at right). It is sewn on a serger and machine-quilted with silver metallic thread from Talon. Folkwear pattern.

Cat's Cradle, *made by Jeanne Elliot, uses appliquéd fake fur, decorative stitches with metallic thread to form braided rug, and free-motion quilting.*

Fishyssoise Coat *uses lamés, novelty fabrics, and all sorts of trims. Both machine strip-piecing and machine-appliqué techniques were used. Hand-beaded and hand-sewn mother-of-pearl buttons. Machine-quilted on Cotton Classic batting from Fairfield Processing Corp.*

Raisa and Nancy Eat Your Heart Out, *designed by Ann Boyce for the 1988 Fairfield Fashion Show. Russian suit with fake-fur trim, blind machine appliqué, and assorted novelty embellishments. Concord House cottons, Cotton Classic batting from Fairfield Processing Corp., metallic thread from Coats. (Slides provided by Fairfield Processing Corp.)*

Wear this comfortable jacket (at right and opposite page) on any occasion—formal or informal. Instructions for patchwork are in Chapter 4. Butterick pattern, machine-pieced with poly-cotton thread and quilted with metallic thread from Coats. Cotton fabrics from Alexander Henry and tissue lamé from Rosebar.

Close-up of haori. Folkwear pattern and black silk noil, China silk flowers, and tissue lamé yo-yo centers.

Free-motion quilting on **Jeweled Butterfly** *quilt. Fabric from Alexander Henry. (Photo courtesy of Quilt World, the House of White Birches. Photo by Nancy Sharp.)*

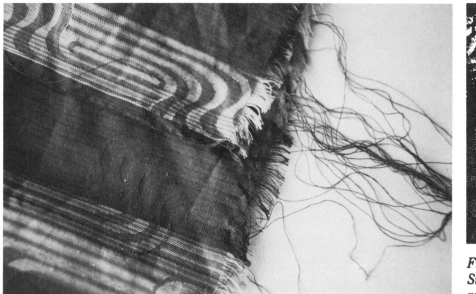

Fig. 2-5:
Silks are easily
raveled.

drawn onto the paper and cut out. The silk shapes can then be later fused onto a background, such as a heavier weight silk or cotton velveteen. The silk appliqués should be machine appliquéd in place with a matching color using machine-embroidery cotton, rayon, or silk thread.

Raveling is not a problem with the thin silks, but the heavier textured silks, such as tussah and raw silk, will ravel (Fig. 2-5). Because these silks are heavier, fusing them for patchwork to prevent raveling makes them too heavy. The edges of the cut-out shapes and strips can be painted with a clear solvent such as Fray Check and left to air-dry. This will both discolor the edges and make them stiff. As an alternative, the edges can be overcast on the sewing machine or serger. However, if

the silk is too loosely woven, these stitches may pull off. If this is the case, overlock these edges again so that they won't pull out. These heavier woven silks can be bonded directly with paper-backed fusible webbing for appliquéing.

Silk noil is available in a wide range of colors. This type of silk is not smooth and silky, but has a woven, nubby texture and a slight sheen. It can be machine-laundered before cutting and is an ideal width (44") for both garments and quilts. It does not need to be lined and the cut edges have a minimum of raveling. Silk noil is about the weight of heavy cotton fabric; it is the same width and is approximately one-third more expensive than good cotton fabric. The colors that are available in silk noil are muted as opposed to the vibrant colors available in

thinner silks and some heavier textured silks. An unlined silk noil garment produces a lot of static electricity when worn, so it should be lined or sprayed with an anti-static fabric spray.

VELVET, VELVETEEN, AND CORDUROY

A fabric has a nap or a pile when you can see fibers sticking up off the fabric's surface. The nap can be seen and felt. Take a piece of corduroy and run your hand down and then up the piece. Do you feel the nap? In one direction, it feels smooth; in the opposite direction, it feels rough. When it is smooth, you are working with the nap or pile; when it is rough, you are working against it.

A nap or pile affects the treatment of the fabric in several ways. First, the color of the fabric changes, depending on the direction of the pile. When the pile runs up from the floor, colors look darker and richer. When the pile runs down, the colors appear brighter and lighter. Second, in a garment, the feel of the fabric is important. The nap or pile must all go in the same direction. If you are working with patchwork, however, the change of color from the different directions of the piles could be an advantage and might be exactly what you wanted to accomplish with your pile fabric. The feel may not be important to you.

Knowing what your fabric can do is integral to its final use. Piles and naps can be wonderful additions to any project. Rich velvets can be luxurious when combined with other fabrics. Knowing how to work with these fabrics makes all the difference when creating patchwork with them.

The most luxurious of all the pile and napped fabrics is velvet. In France, in 1832, Jean Baptiste Martin designed the first double piece velvet loom. Before this time velvet production was a slower process. In Martin's method, fibers are woven in a loop between two layers. The fabric is then split apart with a knife to form two fabrics (Fig. 2-6). The lush pile is the surface result of the splitting process. In contrast,

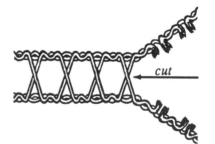

Fig. 2-6:
A double-woven velvet is split apart and a pile results.

velveteen and corduroy are woven on a plain loom. Their pile is formed by looping the crosswise yarns as they weave across the lengthwise yarns. These loops are then cut with wire cutters. Unlike other pile fabrics, velour is knitted. It will stretch and give in all directions, making it a perfect choice for use in sportswear. Pile fabrics with woven backs have either a plain or a twill weave. The twill weave is the strongest.

Velvet may be made from cotton, silk, rayon, or a combination of rayon and acetate. The latter three types of velvets are the most beautiful to look at and to feel. They are also the most difficult to handle. Several companies manufacture velvet and each one has many brand names, confusing the consumer. Suffice it to say, all velvets are not alike. They differ in feel, drapability, handling, sewing, and care. To be safe, determine the fiber content of any velvet you might purchase. This may not be easy because some velvets do not come on bolts. Usually they are hung on metal frames or rolled. Most often they have a tag attached which will tell the fiber content. Write it down when you purchase your piece. Remember to store velvet either rolled or hung while waiting to use. It should not be folded and stacked with your other fabrics.

Velvets are usually woven 39/40" wide. Most pattern yardage charts list fabric requirements for 45"-wide fabric. You will need to convert that difference so that you purchase enough fabric. For example, for 1 yard of 45"- wide, you would need 1-1/8 yard of 40"-wide, and for 4 yards 45"-wide you would need 4-1/2 yards of 40"-wide. In addition, if your pattern does not include a "with nap" layout, you will need to add at least 1/2 to 3/4 yard to the "without nap" amount. You can see that the additional yardage is not a great deal, but it should be considered. On the other hand, don't purchase several yards extra just to be safe because most velvets are expensive and this additional expenditure may not be necessary. If in doubt, ask for help from the store's employee. The store should have a conversion chart available.

Cotton velvet is the easiest to care for and to handle. The cotton velvets are available in rich colors, have a resilient pile, and even more important, are machine-washable and -dryable. They are perfect for children's clothing or for use in patchwork. If you want a washable project, look for Matinee and Street from J.B. Martin. Cotton velvet can be pressed, even on the right side. If the pile gets crushed, it may be brushed back up with no damage.

If you are interested in the most luxurious velvet for dramatic evening wear the silk and rayon velvets have the deepest pile. However, they are not practical for everyday wear.

All pile or napped fabrics require special treatment during the cutting and sewing process. The pile, especially on luxurious velvets, shifts and slides when it is sewn. Velvets (except cotton) must be pressed on a needleboard (Fig. 2-7). A needleboard looks similar to a pet brush, only it is larger and has to set flat on the ironing surface. It is available in sewing stores and by mail order. The inherent problem with using the needleboard is that it is small—usually about a 4" x 10" rectangle. For large pressing jobs, it is not practical. Therefore, as a general rule, use as little ironing as possible with velvet. It crushes too easily.

Velvet can be cut up and used in patchwork to give the project a unique richness. Fusing works for these small amounts of patchwork, but would be cumbersome on a large scale. Use a 100-percent cotton woven interfacing on the back side of the fabric, pressing into a needleboard. The fusing stabilizes the velvet fabric for sewing.

If the velvet is used with no additions, it should be cut in the direction of the pile, if possible. On dresses, it is recommended that the pile run up because it is less likely to mat with friction. A rotary cutter works well with velvets, as do sharp shears. If special

shapes are drawn on the wrong side of the velvet, it should be done carefully and accurately. When a sharpened pencil is used, it damages the pile on the velvet pile side. You can actually see the drawn lines on the right side before it is cut into the pieces.

When sewing velvet on the sewing machine, it is best to:

- Thread the machine with thread a shade darker than the velvet.

- Use mercerized cotton, cotton polyester, or polyester threads.

- Set your stitch length at 2–2.5 or 10–12 stitches per inch.

- Use a #70/10 or #80/12

Fig. 2-7: A needleboard for pressing velvet.

ballpoint or universal needle.

- Pin the pieces to be sewn with thin, sharp silk pins parallel to the border's raw edges.

- Place the heads of the pins facing toward you.

- Place tissue paper underneath the velvet to be sewn to help it pass under the presser foot.

- Loosen the foot pressure if it is not self-adjusting; too much pressure mars the fabric. An even-feed foot is the best foot to sew with, although a roller foot does work.

- Leave the straight pins in the velvet until the last possible moment. The pin's point will slide under the right side of the presser foot and the pin head is pulled out as it approaches the presser foot. Leaving the fabric pinned until this moment minimizes slippage. This also works well when sewing velvet to other fabrics. The resulting sewn seams should be pressed open using the needleboard. The velvet is placed with the pile facing down onto the needleboard. Use a minimal amount of pressing.

Another way to control the even movement of the fabric through the machine is to hold the bottom piece of fabric taut as it moves. Take a few stops at short intervals, leaving the needle in the fabric. Lift the presser foot. This helps the fabric relax and helps prevent shifting.

Seams on velvet projects should not be trimmed closer than 1/4" because the velvet will ravel. It is better to line the project, or wherever there are facings, substitute a lighter weight fabric for the pile fabric to reduce bulk.

Quilting on velvet is a waste of time, especially on a velvet with a long pile. Because of the nap, the shadow effect that quilting provides is lost. It also unevenly mats down the surface and generally is not attractive. Quilting in the ditch or sewn seam is possible, if the fibers of the nap are pushed aside and are not caught up in the stitching. In patchwork garments, if all other areas are quilted, quilting in the ditch would be a suitable choice. A textured metallic thread works well on velvet and will show on the surface. (See section on threads.)

Corduroy, velveteen, and velour are easily used as a base fabric on which to decorate with machine appliqué. Because it has a knit base, velour presents the most problems in

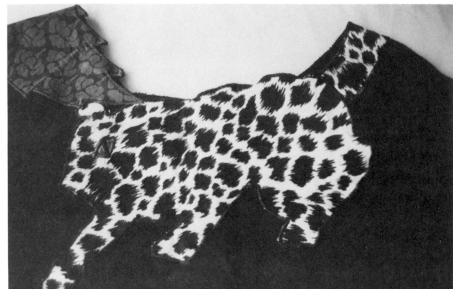

Fig. 2-8:
A velour cat is
appliquéd to
the neckline of
a sweatshirt.

appliqué work. To prevent it from stretching out of shape as you stitch around it, you could fuse it. Then the backing would stabilize and allow you to treat it like any other fabric. Using a tear-off stabilizer will also keep an unfused knit background fabric flat, such as a sweatshirt or velour fabric. Corduroy, velveteen, and velour also have a nap or a one-way cutting direction. This nap provides a shading effect that when used in patchwork is wonderful. In clothing, it is important that the nap all runs in the same direction. For example, if one pant leg were cut with the nap running up and the other running down, your pants would look peculiar. In patchwork, the more shading and coloring differences, the better for the project. This shading becomes an advantage.

In the sewing process, corduroy, velveteen, and velour may be cut, sewn, and quilted like any others (Fig. 2 - 8). Using a serger for piecing will make sewing knit fabrics easier and the bulky seam allowances will be automatically removed. Remember, though, that these napped fabrics are heavier in weight, so that a wall hanging made in corduroys might appear heavy, especially if heavier weight, wide-wale corduroys were used. However, using these fabrics in combination with other fabrics does not present any particular problems. They won't be too heavy.

FAKE FUR

The fake furs being manufactured today are superior to those in the past. They no longer all look fake. We do not see any reason to use real fur to achieve the look, feel, and warmth of real fur when these fabrics can be purchased so readily and at much less cost. They are extremely easy to sew and handle.

Fake fur is a pile fabric that is woven onto a knit backing. When it is cut, it will not ravel; it will, however, shed fibers off of the fur. It can be a little messy to cut and to sew.

If the pile is long, trace around the shapes on the knit backing. Cut carefully around the drawn line in small snips that go only through the knit backing. Be careful not to cut the fur fibers on the top. If you were to cut in a normal fashion, through the whole fabric, you would cut the fur pile unevenly. You can try an X-acto knife or single-edge razor to cut the knit backing if you prefer, but sharp, pointed scissors work well.

One major problem with fake fur is that it will melt if an iron touches it. It can be machine appliquéd, but because it cannot be ironed, fusing is an impossibility. To remedy this, you might use either a spray adhesive (such as No More Pins spray) or a glue stick to secure the appliqué shape in

place. A tear-off stabilizer sheet should be placed underneath the back of the project. The fur pile has to be manually pulled to one side as it is satin stitched in place; otherwise, the fur will get caught up in the stitching and the raw edges may not be satin stitched over.

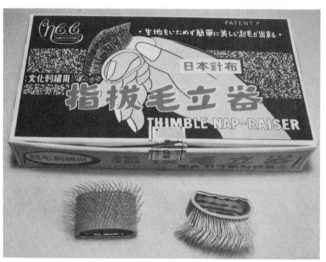

If fake fur is sewn into seam allowances, pull it out carefully using a long straight pin or doll needle, or a little wire brush, called a Bunka brush, that is available in some craft or sewing stores. The wire brush is about 1/2" x 2" long and the metal burrs are made about twice as long as the metal brushes on a velvet needleboard surface (Fig. 2-9). You could purchase a fine wire pet brush if you cannot find this product.

Fig. 2-9: These little brushes can be used on fur to make the nap stand back up after sewing.

You can use fake fur as an accent on a quilted garment, such as for collars and cuffs. It can also be used in accessories, such as hats and muffs.

It is fun to appliqué fake-fur animal shapes, such as dogs, cats, rabbits, jungle animals, and mice, on a project. The animals can be embellished with jeweled collars and plastic eyes. A fabric glue will work well with these fabrics. (Some of the thinner velour fabrics can be substituted for furs. Velour fabrics can be ironed and they are easy to fuse for machine appliqué.)

SATINS AND SATIN–LIKE FABRICS

Satins are generally made from synthetic materials such as acetates, although they were originally made of silk. Unfortunately, these silks tend to deteriorate with age (Fig. 2-10). They have a high shine to them and are extremely effective in patchwork and appliqué work. Many fabrics can be woven with the satin weave, but not all are satins. Satins can be soft as well as stiff and heavy. They can have a bright or dull sheen.

Because of the way satin is woven, it requires special attention when it is cut and sewn up into projects. The major problem with this fabric is that it ravels and frays. It snags and is easily marked by pins or rough surfaces, including your sewing machine's feed dogs. After the satin is cut apart, particularly in small strips and pieces, it needs to have the edges treated. If the edges are either zigzagged or serged, this will help prevent or cut down on the amount of raveling. This fabric does not ravel nearly as much as lamés, but it can be disastrous in patchwork, particularly when using 1/4" seam allowances.

Fig. 2-10: This antique quilt shows how satins deteriorate with age.

Another way to treat the edges is to paint them with liquid sealants and place them on waxed paper to air dry. This will both discolor the fabric and stiffen it. This is fine when the treated edges are sewn into seam allowances. Otherwise, these edges are covered with satin stitches in machine appliqué.

With no edge treatment, the fabrics can be cut and sewn into seam allowances only if every sewn seam is to be quilted over. The quilting stitches will lock in the sewn seams. The unquilted patchwork should be handled carefully until it is quilted to prevent the fabrics from fraying.

This shiny and slippery fabric is slick on the back side. When it is fused with all types of synthetic and woven cotton fusible interfacings, the interfacings will not adhere to the back side of the fabric. They will seem to stick, but in handling, they will pull off.

Another problem, particularly with solid-colored and smooth-textured satins, is that they water spot. You must not spray them with a water bottle when ironing them. Iron them carefully with a dry iron or a professional steam iron.

If satins are carefully handled, they are effective when used with different fabrics or by themselves.

A technique for mixing up fabrics of different properties, such as silks, velvets, corduroys, and satins is to piece them together with a serger. This machine accommodates different fabric textures and thicknesses. The overlocking threads seal in the edges and sew the fabrics together evenly. On a sewing machine use an even-feed foot to accommodate fabric variances.

For machine appliquéing, while fusible interfacings will not stick to satins, iron-on, paper-backed fusible webbings will. Iron the rough, nonpaper side of the paper onto the wrong side of the satin with a dry iron. Do not use steam.

Then draw the desired shapes onto the paper side of the fabric (Fig. 2-11) and cut them out. Peel the paper off later, before fusing. Do not pin these pieces onto the project—the pin holes will show on the satin. This arrangement should be laid out on an ironing board. This will keep the pieces together until

Fig. 2-11: Draw shape on fused side of paper with pencil. Peel off paper, place in position, and iron in place.

they are fused in place. Fuse the arranged pieces in place with a dry iron. Unlike other fabrics that are fused, these satin pieces should be covered with a thin, dry press cloth to fuse them in place; otherwise, the fusible webbing will leak out around the edges onto the iron's surface. This seems to happen most when fusing satin in place, rather than with other fabrics.

The easiest way to seal the raw edges of the satin appliqué is to use a nonsewing method of painting the edges with fabric paints. They are manufactured in all colors and sheens. Some are glitter-colored and provide an interesting sheen.

But the best method for appliquéing satin in place is to use machine appliqué (Fig. 2-12). Set your machine for a close satin stitch at a desired width. If the length of the stitches is too close, the stitches will pile up and cause a lump. Use rayon thread on top and regular thread in a matching color in the bobbin. The bobbin can be threaded with rayon thread, but it is not seen and it is more expensive to use; therefore it is an unnecessary expenditure. A matching color of rayon thread blends in well with the satin appliqué.

After stitching, press the stitched appliqué on the wrong side of the project. This gives the finished appliqué section a flat, professional look.

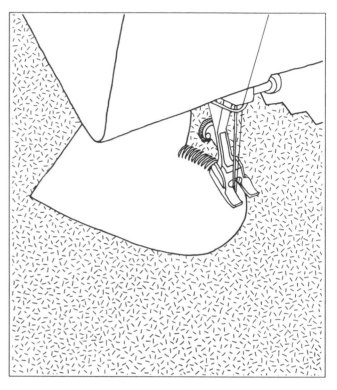

Fig. 2-12: Machine appliqué around shape with satin stitch.

Satin fabric should be rolled up on a cardboard fabric tube, if possible, when not in use, but don't pin the cut raw edge in place. Pin holes show in satin because of the high thread count. Don't use tape either. An extra piece of bias tape or a strip of fabric tied around the tube in a couple of places will hold the fabric on the tube. When folded, especially for long periods of time, the fold lines in satin tend to become permanent. In addition, if exposed to light, like other fabrics, satins fade very quickly.

Fig. 2-13: Shadow quilting can be done by machine as well as by hand. Stitching done on a Pfaff 1473 CD.

SEE–THROUGH FABRICS

When thin, transparent fabrics are used in patchwork, they should be backed with another fabric. Otherwise, the fabric is too sheer, and when it is sewn onto another fabric, the seam allowances will show through. If the project is to have batting underneath, the batting will also show through.

Shadow quilting is a common technique that uses see-through fabrics (Fig. 2-13). This technique is used in quilting and French hand sewing. It sandwiches appliqué shapes between an underneath fabric and a top layer of see-through fabric, such as organdy. The three layers are stitched through by hand or machine, following the raw edges of the appliqué shapes. The see-through fabric mutes the colors of the appliqué pieces. Metallic fabrics can be used for appliqué as well. This

would provide a dull luster instead of a shiny luster.

Shadow quilting can also be used with laces, either on the top or in between a sheer top and solid bottom layer. Sew both layers together in the seam allowances as one fabric. The upper fabric is loose against the lower fabric, but usually both fabrics are tightly woven and there is not much play in both the fabrics.

A different method for handling see-through fabrics is to fuse the upper fabric to the underneath fabric with a paper-backed fusible webbing. Dry-iron the rough (or glued) side of the paper to the right side of the underneath fabric. After the paper-ironed fabric has cooled, peel the paper off. Then place the see-through fabric on top of the underneath fabric and dry-iron to it. The fusible webbing will melt and

fuse the two fabrics together. It will not bleed through the see-through fabric onto the iron. The resulting double-fused fabric is now a new single fabric. It will be a little stiff in texture, but it can be easily sewn into seam allowances. A slight light-colored residue remains, which lightens the darker underneath fabric. A black fabric, for example, will appear gray.

LACES AND SPECIALTY FABRICS

Lace can be used to add beauty and texture to patchwork and appliqué. Its elegant nature makes it suitable more for formal than everyday wear. The addition of lace or lace fabrics to your projects adds a special touch that cannot be duplicated by other fabrics.

Lace is available to the consumer in yardage as well as in trim. The laces available in

yardage vary from simple woven laces to heavily hand-beaded and sequined laces that are used in evening and bridal gowns. The specialty hand-embroidered and beaded laces retail for as high as several hundred dollars a yard. If you are not absolutely sure of your sewing skills, you probably wouldn't purchase such expensive material. Just cutting into it could be stressful.

Most home sewers would be looking for a less expensive alternative to these beautiful but expensive laces. Of course, it is possible to hand bead and hand embroider less expensive laces yourself. If time is not a problem, you might want to try this. Beads can be applied by machine to save time and money in purchasing similar ready-made fabrics (Fig. 2-14; see Chapter 3 on embellishments). In a pinch, beads and pearls can be glued onto the

Fig. 2-14: Vest section shows pearls on twill tape enclosed in the collar. Patchwork construction in process. Laces by Wyle-Weiner.

Fig. 2-15: An old piece of lace was inserted over a darker piece of fabric for embellishment. The darker color shows through the lace.

lace. Glues, such as Glu 'N Wash by Plaid Industries, are made for this purpose.

Economical laces are generally made from a blend of fibers. They can be inexpensive and are available in the bridal section of fabric stores. These laces are machine-woven with lots of open spaces in the fabric. Therefore, they cannot be fused underneath; the fusible will bleed through onto the iron or outer surfaces. This fabric needs to have a lining placed underneath—either a shiny fabric, such as satin or moiré, or a nonshiny fabric such as cotton. Since these laces are available in a large array of colors, ranging from pastels to jewel colors, using a contrasting color as a lining can give a totally different look (Fig. 2-15); the lace patterns will show on a contrast fabric, but will blend in on a matching color.

Ruffled eyelet laces and trims are made from cotton and cotton blends. There are also many decorative laces made from heavy cotton thread. These laces usually have a binding on one edge and that edge needs to be sewn into the seam allowance. These trims are used in crafts, quilts, and garments. A few of the ruffled laces can be topstitched onto the outside of a project if the ruffled edges are finished edges and don't need to be enclosed.

When unlined laces are used in patchwork, the seam allowances of the unlined lace have to be pressed toward the surrounding patchwork pieces. Otherwise, the seam allowances will show through the lace. If the lace is lined and both the lining and the lace are used as one fabric, the seams do not have to be pressed outward.

Sewing laces and lace trims onto surrounding fabrics is easy with a serger. Thread the serger in the color of the lace and set it up with a rolled edge foot. Connect the lace to the edge of the fabric, with no bulk or seam allowances. This is an updated French hand sewing method.

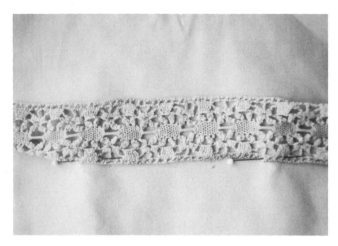

Fig. 2-16: Pin edges to background with a stabilizer underneath, then satin stitch.

Lace trims can also be cut into individual decorative motifs and sewn onto a background fabric in several ways. The lace is pinned down to the backing fabric around the motifs desired. The outside edges of the lace are satin stitched along the outside edge of the lace trim. They could be straight stitched but that would leave obvious cut edges.

1. Thread the sewing machine with a color to match the lace and set it for a narrow, close satin stitch.

2. Use an open-toed or plastic appliqué foot for good visibility.

3. Place a piece of tear-off stabilizer on the wrong side of the background fabric to keep the stitching flat and smooth (Fig. 2-16).

4. After all the edges of the lace are satin stitched onto the background, pull off the stabilizer from the backing fabric (Fig. 2-17).

Fig. 2-17: Cut away background material from behind strip.

5. With small, sharp-pointed embroidery scissors, cut the background material away from behind the appliquéd lace strips inside the sewn satin stitches. This will make the lace strip see-through. Figure 2-18 shows the finished effect.

Fig. 2-18: Finished lace insertion.

The same lace insertion technique is also used for lace yardage in French hand sewing. On a garment, however, the placement of the lace must be considered on the person's body. Be careful where you place see-through areas.

To insert individual lace motifs in a window-like or reverse appliqué setting:

1. Draw the opening or shape on a piece of facing fabric.

Fig. 2-19: Draw design on facing and pin facing to background. Straight stitch around drawn line and cut away center.

2. Pin this to the lace fabric and straight stitch on the drawn line.

3. Cut away the center and clip curves (Fig. 2-19).

4. Turn the facing through to the wrong side and press flat.

5. If the background fabric is sheer, trim the facing excess to 1/4" from the sewn edge.

6. Pin larger-than-the-opening piece of lace in the center of

the opening, pinning around the faced edge.

7. Use a blind hem stitch on the machine to stitch around the edge of the faced opening (Fig. 2-20). The straight stitches of the blind hem

Fig. 2-20: Turn facing to underneath and place lace on top of tear-off stabilizer; blind hem stitch around opening from right side.

stitches barely fall onto the lace background and the left swing of the needle barely catches the faced background edge. Figure 2-21 shows the finished lace insertion.

Fig. 2-21: The finished lace heart insertion.

Fig. 2-22:
*Draw heart
shape on back
of fabric and
cut out on
drawn line.*

4. Next satin stitch over these straight stitches and the raw edges; remove the tear-off backing (Fig. 2-24).

Laces with pearls, beads, and sequins presewn onto them have to be carefully cut and sewn. The fabric should be taped with wide masking tape along the cutting line, and cut down the center. Both halves of the masking tape remain after the cutting is done. This

A similar method does not face the opening:

1. Cut the opening the exact size of the motif (Fig. 2-22).

2. Place lace under the opening and a piece of tear-off backing product behind both fabrics on the wrong side.

3. First straight stitch the layers together around the edge of the opening (Fig. 2-23).

holds the beads and sequins onto the fabric as much as possible. It also keeps them from flying into the air or into your eyes.

Fig. 2-24:
*Satin stitch
over straight
stitch and tear-
away
stabilizer.*

Fig. 2-23:
*Place stabilizer
and lace under
cut-out section
and straight
stitch raw edge
in place.*

Fig. 2-25:
A piece of
sequinned
fabric.

Sew these fabrics together carefully and slowly (Fig. 2-25). The most tedious but easiest method is to remove the jewels and beads from the seam allowance area before it is sewn together. After sewing the seams, the jewels and beads are then hand sewn back in places where they have come off on the finished sewn edge. For comfort, the inside seam allowance should be free of beads or jewels. The sewn seam allowances need to be finished off, either with an overlocked edge or with a seam-edge covering such as Seams Great.

All the jeweled and beaded fabrics have to be handled carefully. The sequins cannot be ironed because the heat will dull and melt them. These fabrics are expensive and require special dry cleaning methods.

The alternative to sequinned fabrics is fabric that has sequin discs, with no holes, fused onto the background. The fabric fusing technique creates one complete fabric when it is manufactured. Usually the background is a sheer organdy, most often silk, and the fabric needs a lining as with shadow quilting.

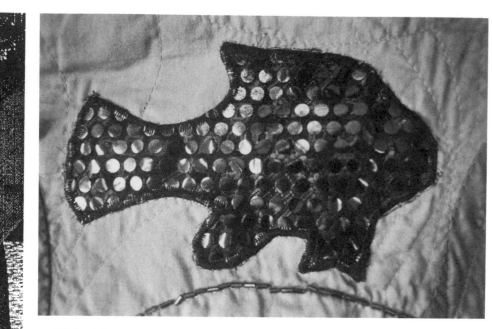

Fig. 2-26: Close-up of sequin discs fused on background fabric used as a fish shape on a garment. The sequins appear to be scales on the fish. This fabric retailed for $140/yard.

This fabric can be cut out in any motif, through the fused sequins. It can be machine appliquéd onto a project to add shimmer and texture and glitz. It can be used as scales on a fish (Fig. 2-26), spotted lily flowers, etc. It can be sewn with a #80/12 needle and will not ravel or chip the sequins.

sive, ranging between $75 and $150 per yard (Fig. 2-27).

If you are buying expensive beaded and jeweled laces, be sure to practice stitching on a very small swatch before actually working with it in your project. Sometimes the employees of shops that sell these materials can give good advice on working with them. Be sure to seek any advice that is available before using expensive fabrics.

THE REAL GLITTER— LAMÉS

Lamé fabrics add glitter and glamor when used with nonglittery fabrics (Fig. 2-28). When used in patchwork and appliqué, these fabrics can spark up all other surrounding fabrics. Because several types of lamés are available, we will cover each one individually. When choosing to use lamé fabrics in your work, be sure to

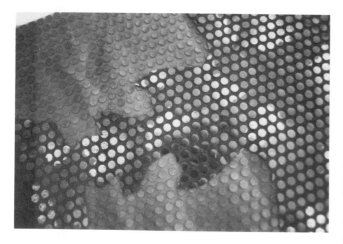

Fig. 2-27: Sample of the fabric used in the fish shape above.

Available in specialty stores, the fabrics can be purchased in several combinations of colors. Like beaded fabric, it is expen-

Fig. 2-28: A variety of silver and black patterned and plain lamés. Fabric courtesy of Hyman Hendler.

ask yourself the following questions before making your choices:

- What will the project be used for?

- Will it require frequent washings?

- Will it be exposed to extreme heat?

- Will it be exposed to a great deal of light?

- Are you planning to hand quilt your item?

- How much money do you want to spend?

Tricot lamé is the easiest type of lamé to sew. This lamé is made by imprinting a metallic color onto a 54"-wide knit base. It is heavier than other lamés and can be used as it is purchased with no added stabilizers.

Tricot lamé scraps can be used the same way as leather, suede, synthetic suede, or other leather-type scraps. Because they don't ravel, every inch of these fabrics can be used, with no waste. They do not have a grain that will stretch, although they may have directional limitations because of nap or color reflections. If cut in different directions, the metallic color changes. Tricot lamé does have some give to it because of its knit backing, so when piecing in patchwork, it should be handled carefully.

Tricot lamé is nearly twice the price of tissue lamé. However, it is wider, so you get more fabric in a yard, and it doesn't require any additional treatment before using it pieced in patchwork. Taking those things into consideration, tricot lamé could be less expensive to use in the long run. A thinner grade of tricot lamé is available and is generally less expensive than the thicker grades.

Because tricot lamé is made by applying metallic color to a knit background, it will not wear as well as a woven lamé. The metallic surface will rub off, especially at wear points, seams, and edges. The color will dull and adhere to a hot iron's plate if it is pressed directly with no press cloth. Tricot lamé should not be ironed on a high setting.

The quilt *I Got Lucky* (see color pages) uses tricot-backed lamé. Although we caution you about the effect ironing could have on the fabric, the pieces in this quilt were ironed directly. The iron setting was low, and before the actual patchwork was ironed, samples of the fabric were tested. Because the resulting quilt was a wall hanging, it would not receive the wear and tear of a garment or a quilt that would be used and washed often.

Several seams were redone due to sewing errors, with no apparent damage. The holes made by the stitches seemed to blend back into the original fabric.

If you want to use tricot lamé in an appliquéd project, there are two methods to try:

(1) satin-stitch appliqué
(2) blind or invisible appliqué

1. Satin-stitch appliqué:

- First, zigzag or satin stitch by machine. Use a #80/12 needle.

- To prepare tricot lamé for appliqué, place the lamé with the metallic side down (wrong side facing up).

- Cut a piece of fusible web paper such as Wonder-Under or Magic Fuse smaller than the fabric. The rough side of the paper should be against the wrong side of the fabric. This rough side contains the fusible webbing. When it is heat activated, it will melt onto any surface.

- Dry-iron the paper onto the wrong side of the tricot lamé.

- Trace the shape of the appliqué onto the pressed-on-paper side of the tricot lamé.

- With scissors, cut the drawn shapes out of the fused lamé.

- After the shapes have been cut out, peel off the paper to expose the fused web on the wrong side of the lamé. The remaining piece will feel rubbery.

- Arrange the shapes on the background fabric. It is important not to place pins in edges that will not be satin stitched over. The little holes made by the pins may otherwise show on the right side of the lamé in your finished project.

- Carefully cover the arranged appliqué shapes with a clean, dry press cloth. Place the iron on top of the press-cloth and leave it in place a few seconds, then lift the iron and move it to a new section.

- Do not slide the iron back and forth on the press cloth, as this action might make the appliqué pieces shift or wrinkle. If the pieces do not seem to be solidly fused, repeat the process with a damp press cloth. An iron that does not have enough steam may not yield enough moisture to make the fabric adhere. A damp press cloth will help with this problem.

- When the fused section is ready for appliqué, place a piece of tear-off stabilizer on the wrong side of the background fabric. The stabilizer can be pinned through on the background, not the lamé, about every six inches with #1 safety pins so that the stabilizer fabric will not shift. For the satin-stitch appliqué method, please refer to the metallic thread section beginning on page 23.

Fig. 2-29:
Draw design
shape on back
of tricot lamé.

2. Blind or invisible appliqué with turned edges:

- Trace around the appliqué shape on the wrong side of the tricot lamé (Fig. 2-29). Leave an inch of space between the drawn lines. Use a nonsmearing ballpoint pen (a Cross pen does well). A pencil will catch and pick on the fabric and it is hard to see the drawn lines. If you are working on a darker color, a water-soluble blue pen would work well. Do not use a purple disappearing marker unless you work quickly, as it will disappear in several hours.

- Place a second piece of tricot lamé underneath the traced fabric with right sides together. Pin together the background at this point. Do not pin inside the drawn shapes. Pin outside them.

Leave 1" between all drawn lines.

- Set the sewing machine to a normal stitch length: 2–2.5 or 10–12 stitches to the inch.

- Sew around all drawn lines so they are all completely stitched. Do not leave any openings.

- Cut apart all the shapes about 1/8" outside all the stitched lines. Clip off out side corners to just outside the sewn edge. Clip the inside corners and around the curved edges.

Fig. 2-30: Slit center back of one shape, and turn to right side. Because it is tricot lamé, it should not be touched with the iron without a press cloth.

the scissors can be inserted in the piece to make the slit. Cut the opening large enough so that the piece can be turned inside out. Lightly finger-press the edges to turn them under. If the piece needs ironing, put a press cloth over it. The edges will not press perfectly flat because this type of lamé will not hold a crisp crease (Fig. 2-31).

- You can then either hand appliqué the piece in place or machine blind hem in place with matching metallic thread (Fig. 2-32).

- Carefully pull apart and slit the sewn and clipped shape in the center on one wrong side of the fabric (Fig. 2-30). Tricot lamé tends to stick together so it is helpful to carefully use a straight pin to pull away the center of the back of the lamé backing so that the sharp tip of

Fig. 2-31: Finished shape will not be flat and smooth. Try to pull out points and flatten as best you can.

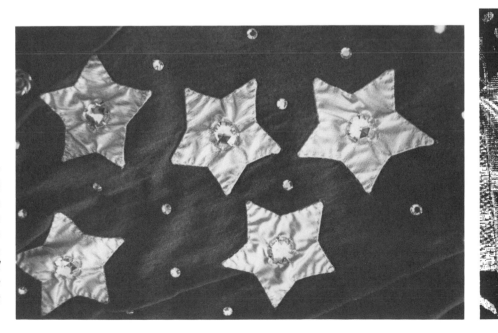

Fig. 2-32: Tricot lamé stars are shown appliquéd to the bodice of a purchased dress. Notice the rhinestones in the center.

When tricot lamé is used as an accent in patchwork, the lamé can be cut into strips or patchwork pieces with shears or a rotary cutter. If you have a serger, it can be used for cutting strips as well. Remove the needle threads and feed fabric through the blade. The lamé pieces can be sewn onto other fabrics used in the patchwork. It can be sewn with normal sewing thread of your choice and doesn't need any special handling. It can also be serged together with other fabrics. As explained earlier, any pressing has to be done through a press cloth. For small patchwork, this can be a little tricky. You need to finger press the seams open or to one side and quickly place the press cloth over it. It can then be pressed, but as mentioned before, the seams will not be as sharp or flat as those with cotton fabrics or other types of lamé.

Tissue lamé can be one of the most effective accents on patchwork and appliqué projects. With the methods of preparation explained, it can be easy and economical to sew. Its preparation is determined by how the fabric is used.

Tissue lamé is a woven metallic fabric manufactured in Japan. Available in a 42" width, it comes in a wider range of colors than other types of lamés. Because this type of lamé is actually manufactured with a woven metallic fiber, the sheen is brighter, with more intensity, than an applied color such as tricot lamé.

Tissue lamé is also available in many prints: floral, striped, checked, swirled, and more. These designs are printed on top of the tissue lamé. For example, a tissue lamé printed with pink roses is made by printing pink roses onto a gold tissue lamé base.

Checks and plaids, however, are woven designs.

Tissue lamé is relatively affordable in comparison to other lamé fabrics. It generally retails in about the same price range as 100-percent cotton fabrics ($4 to $8 per yard, depending on where it is purchased).

Tissue lamé has one universal disadvantage—it ravels when cut on the straight of grain. There are several remedies for this problem, but do not think that cutting a larger seam allowance will prevent raveling; it will eventually ravel into the sewn seam and cannot be repaired easily once this has happened.

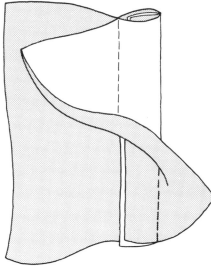

Fig. 2-33: French seam.

One problem-solving technique is to machine-finish the cut edges in two steps. If the lamé is only overcast (zigzagged) on the machine or overlocked on the serger, it will not keep the edges from raveling. The overlocked threads on the edge will pull off the edge of the fabric. The sewn (overcast) seam needs to be turned under a second time and run through the machine again. If a serger is used, it also needs to be run through a second time. Even when the rolled edge is stitched on a serger, it must be repeated a second time as well.

This technique can also be expanded into a sewn French seam on tissue lamé when used in a garment (Fig. 2-33). Encasing a seam within another seam is a good way to finish an edge that might ravel with wear. In garment construction, this seam finish makes the inside of the garment as neat as the outside.

A French seam is best suited for use with lightweight and sheer fabrics because no raw edges show through. The finished seam looks like a plain seam on the right side of the finished project and on the back it appears as if a tuck has been taken in the fabric.

Begin a French seam by stitching the wrong sides of the fabric together. If you are making a garment and the seam allowance is important, be sure that this first line of stitching is half of the seam allowance. When stitching is complete, turn project to the wrong side and press and stitch seam again on seam allowance line. Be sure that you have enclosed inside of this seam all of the seam stitched previously.

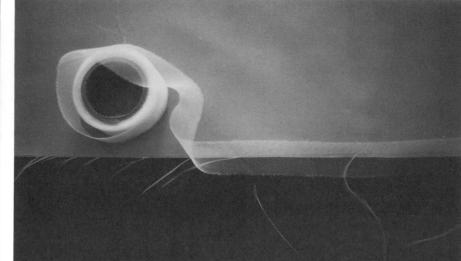

Fig. 2-34: Seams Great is used to finish edges.

The French seam is not suitable for use on bias edges but makes a perfect finish for straight seams where there is a chance that raveling may occur. If the seam is very long, puckering may occur if attention is not given to prevent it when stitching. This finish is perfect for use on fabrics that might cause itching due to scratchy fibers. If very sheer fabrics are used, you might want to cover the feed dogs to prevent them from pulling the fabric down inside.

Another method of finishing off a raw edge, particularly on a garment edge, is to use a product called Seams Great (Fig. 2-34). This is a tricot tape that is loosely zigzagged onto the fabric edge. When the tape is pulled, it curls under naturally. Turn the other edge of the Seams Great over the raw edge and zigzag it into place,

catching both sides at once. Seams Great can also be folded over the edge of the lamé and zigzagged over. The excess Seams Great can be trimmed off. This will help eliminate scratchiness.

Another method to finish off lamé's raw edges is to use a clear sealant such as Fray Check. The sealant does not wash out if laundered and it does not flake off with handling. The easiest way to use this product is to paint a thin line of the sealant onto the raw, cut edges. Place the painted lamé onto a piece of waxed paper to air-dry. When this sealant is used, it will discolor the tissue lamé's edges. If it is used on an edge of a patchwork strip or piece, the treated edge will be sewn into the seam allowance.

This is fine for an edge of tissue lamé used in patchwork that will not be next to skin. Otherwise, it would be extremely uncomfortable and itchy since when it is dry, it is stiff. Choose this technique with an eye to your time; it is tedious to paint many patchwork pieces.

The easiest solution for using tissue lamé in patchwork is to fuse the fabric with preshrunk 100-percent woven cotton interfacing. This interfacing is used in garment work, particularly in shirt collars. Regular synthetic fusibles will not stick to the lamé. It is easy to fuse the tissue lamé to the 100-percent cotton fusible interfacing. The tissue lamé can be directly ironed, as opposed to the tricot lamé, which requires a cloth covering. The interfacing to be fused should be cut slightly smaller than the tissue lamé. When fusing the fabrics, you may want to use a damp press cloth if using a conventional home iron. Do not fuse the interfacing as specified in the manufacturer's directions; if the iron is on the lamé too long, the lamé will melt and crinkle. Move the iron quickly around the fabric until the fabric is all fused. If bubbles appear on the lamé after it is fused, you probably didn't preshrink the fusible (Fig. 2-35). Repeated ironing will fuse those spots. This can also be repeated after the lamé is cut up into pieces and sewn together with other fabrics.

Do not try to fuse the lamé with a Teflon ironing sheet. The heat that is generated from its use is too high and it will melt the fibers on the lamé.

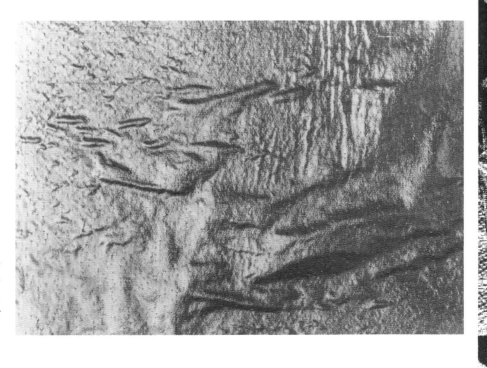

Fig. 2-35: Air bubbles may form on lamé during fusing.

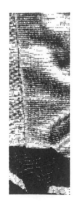

Fig. 2-36: A no-sew way to finish edges is to fuse the design to the surface and glitter-paint around edges. This sweatshirt design used a tulip print from Alexander Henry.

Once the tissue lamé is fused, it can be cut up into shapes and strips exactly like a 100-percent cotton fabric. The fusing of the lamé makes the tissue lamé opaque and the resulting fused fabric is about the same weight as a good 100-percent cotton. It can be sewn and ironed exactly like a 100-percent cotton fabric. However, when using lamé in this manner, the sewn garment or quilt should be dry cleaned and not machine washed. The manufacturers of tissue lamé suggest dry cleaning methods only. When tissue lamé is used in sweatshirt appliqué, many people find it launders well. Laundering fused fabric can make the fabric separate, however. We recommend dry cleaning where fusibles are used.

Tissue lamé can also be fused with a paper-backed fusible webbing when it is being prepared for machine appliqué. This is the easiest method for this type of machine work. The cut-out shape with the paper peeled off can be directly ironed onto the background. It later can be satin stitched over with a shiny thread such as metallic or rayon (see pages 23 and 28 on thread). A jiffy nonsew method of finishing off the edges is to paint the raw appliqué edge with a glitter paint to lock in the edges after fusing the pieces in place. The fusible combined with the glitter paint will prevent raveling and hold the piece in place (Fig. 2-36). This technique may be used with most fabrics, including tissue lamé.

If the edges are turned under on a tissue lamé fused with 100-percent cotton interfacing, it will generally produce a thick edge, too bulky and cumbersome for hand or machine blind appliqué. Instead, cut an unfused appliqué piece or shape 1/4" larger than the finished size and paint a clear sealant around the edge. For hand appliqué, turn under edges, although they will be a little stiff. At least you will not have to quilt through a second layer of cotton interfacing under the lamé.

Tissue lamé is a wonderful fabric to use when cut on the bias. Bias strips of tissue lamé will not ravel. The strips can be pulled through a bias tape maker and ironed directly for use as bias finishes. The finished, turned-under bias tape can then be rolled onto a cardboard tube for later use. If lamé is used as a bias edge, remember that it is a more delicate fabric than cotton and

may not wear as well. Thus it should not be used as an edge finish on a garment that will be worn daily. (See page 114 on bias tapes.)

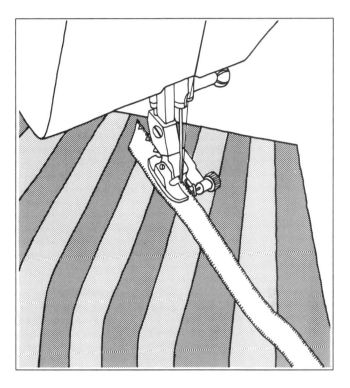

The bias strips can be blind appliquéd onto a background with matching metallic thread for use in stems or other design motifs that require thin, curving strips (Fig. 2-37).

Fig. 2-37: Tissue lamé bias being blind appliquéd.

Woven-fabric-backed lamé is the most brilliant of the lamés. It is also the most difficult to sew and is too fragile for long-term wear. The metallic fibers are woven and bonded onto a woven fabric backing. This lamé contains thicker metallic threads, but the lengthwise metallic threads are more susceptible to both snags and breakage during sewing and through normal wear and tear (Fig. 2-38). The metallic fibers can be pulled away from the backing fabric, and the fabric is also very ravelly when it is cut apart. The best method to remedy this problem is to cut out the piece to be sewn and paint the entire surface with a clear sealant. This should be done on a piece of waxed paper and left to air-dry.

For a garment that will have a lot of wear, this type of lamé should not be used. Even if it is well prepared, it does not wear well on a garment. Although this fabric is used mainly in theatrical costumes, the brilliant metallic colors are tempting to use artistically and sometimes worth the trouble on a wall hanging or a garment worn only on special occasions. The fibers will still break loose and eventually fall out, leaving the underneath bonding fabric exposed.

The lamé color will darken slightly, but painting the entire piece with clear sealant will make it a consistent color and seal in all the threads.

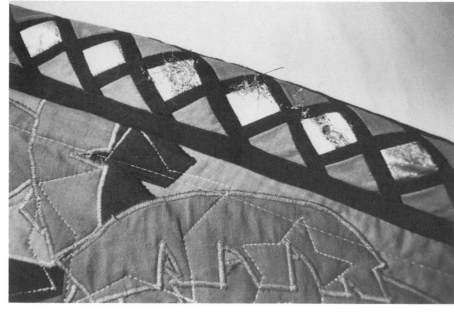

Fig. 2-38: Woven-backed lamé has frayed down to backing on Saw Grass Fire *coat.*

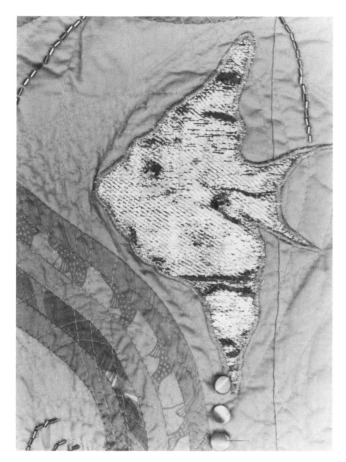

Fig. 2-39: Close-up of machine appliqué with woven-backed lamé and crystal beads.

Woven-fabric-backed lamé can be appliquéd with a satin stitch in the same manner as tissue lamé (Fig. 2-39). As in patchwork, the appliqué shapes should be placed only in an area that will not have much abrasion or wear.

There are a few other novelty lamé fabrics:

- Tissue lamé with soft flocked motifs fused onto it.

- Prewrinkled and crushed tissue lamé that should not be fused. It is sewn as it is, and the edges can be sealed by a clear sealant or by overcasting the edges as described in the tissue lamé section. Both of these fabrics retail for the same approximate price as regular tissue lamé.

- A black-warp tissue lamé is also available in a limited number of colors. This type of lamé appears darker in value than the regular tissue lamé. A woven brocade lamé is an example of black-warp lamé.

- The most expensive is a lamé of silk threads mixed with metallic threads. It has the same general appearance as tissue lamé, but it has a softer hand and a softer, richer color. It retails for about three times the price of tissue lamé.

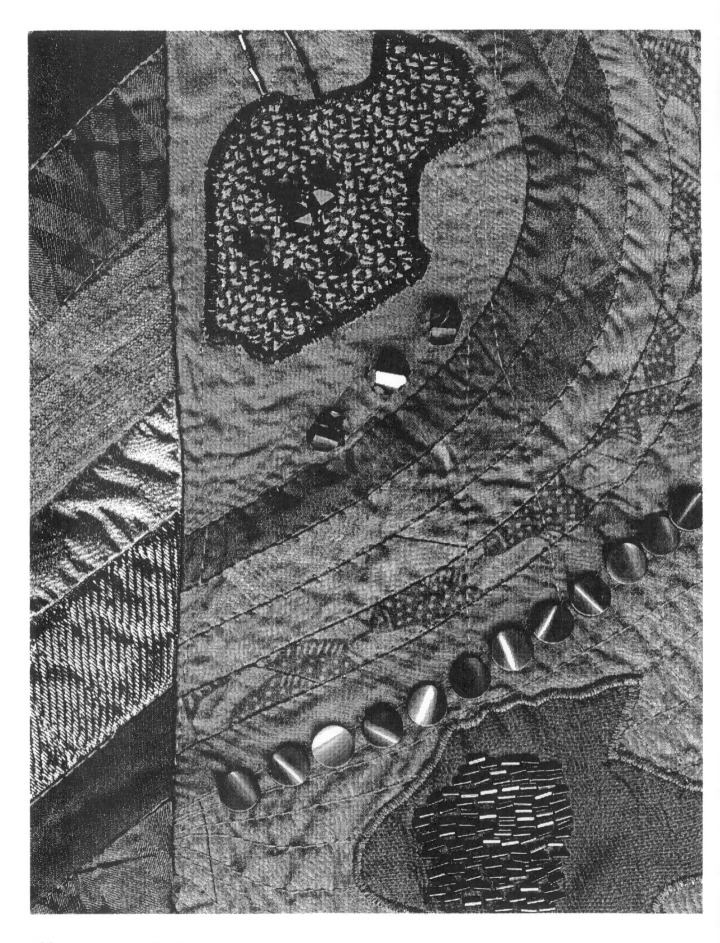

EMBELLISHMENTS 3

Figs. 3-1: Embellishments that can be added by machine.

Once a project is completed in patchwork, appliqué, or quilting, it can then be further embellished with any number of objects to add texture, color, glitz, and interest (Figs. 3-1, 3-2).

Depending on how much time and money you want to spend on the project, you can make an ordinary project spectacular with the addition of a few well-placed embellishments.

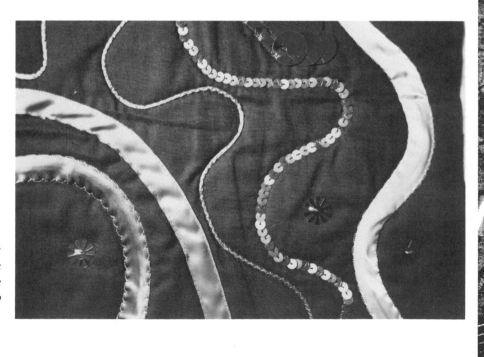

Figs. 3-2: Embellishments that can be added by machine.

SHISHA MIRRORS

Fig. 3-3: Shisha mirrors.

Shisha mirrors are small disks about the size of a quarter (Figs. 3-3, 3-4). They originated in India and are often an integral part of surface design in that country. Traditionally, the antique-type mirrors are made of thin glass that has lots of imperfections and bubbles on the surface. As a rule, they are not fragile and will not break easily. Imported from India, they are available in trim stores and by mail order. The surface of most antique-type shisha mirrors is a much darker silver than a new mirror surface. Some are available in rainbow colors that resemble the colors of automobile oil that has leaked onto pavement.

You can also buy regular cut glass (contemporary) shisha mirrors. The glass is heavier and is about the clarity and thickness of the mirrors that are used in makeup compacts. Although thicker, contemporary shishas are much less durable and do not have the charm of the antique-type shisha mirrors.

Shisha mirrors are available in a variety of shapes. They are traditionally circular, but they can also be purchased in other shapes, such as triangles and squares. Antique-type shishas can be machine-washed, but newer, clearer glass cannot. Shisha mirrors are an exception to the quilt-first rule. They have to be added into an appliqué motif or applied to the surface before it is batted or lined.

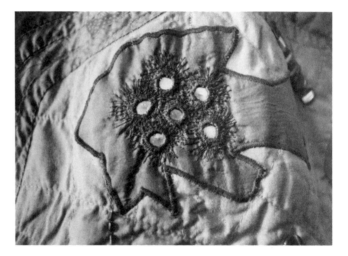

The easiest way to apply shisha mirrors is to purchase the shisha mirrors that are sold with companion metal findings similar to that of metal studs. The shisha mirror stud finding has a circular metal opening that holds the shisha mirror. The underneath metal prongs are punched through the base fabric and pressed flat by either needle-nose pliers or the flat metal end of a screwdriver (Fig. 3-5).

Fig. 3-4: Close-up of shisha on fish coat.

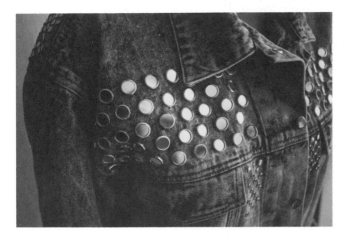

and easier. Any zigzag machine can accomplish this:

1. Mark shisha openings on the fabric, making them smaller than the shisha mirror.

2. Pin a piece of tear-off stabilizer underneath the area to be worked. This will both stabilize the fabric and keep the machine stitches even.

3. With the sewing machine, straight stitch inside the drawn lines about 1/8" smaller than the drawn line (Fig. 3-6). You can do this with the feed dogs up or down. (See Chapter 1, On Top of the Glitz.)

Fig. 3-5: Commercial mirror studs may be used to replace shisha mirrors. This purchased jacket has been covered with these mirror studs.

A second method of attaching shisha uses an embroidered plastic or bone ring as a frame over the mirror. Using a thread at least as heavy as topstitching thread or pearl cotton, embroider with a blanket stitch over the ring until it is entirely covered. Use a shisha mirror slightly larger than the embroidered ring. Then stitch the embroidered ring onto the background surface around the outside edges so that the mirror is sandwiched between the ring and the background surface.

You can also purchase a hand-embroidered shisha ring by mail order, a distinct time saver (see our Source List). This is not available in many colors.

Hand embroidering the openings and surrounding opening surface of shisha mirrors is time-consuming. Fortunately, a sewing machine alternative developed by Caryl Rae Hancock makes this embellishment much faster

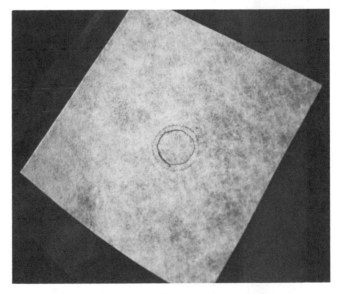

- With the feed dogs up, the presser foot must be constantly lifted to turn the fabric. So that you can see what you

Fig. 3-6: Trace shisha shape onto tear-off stabilizer and stitch inside drawn line.

Fig. 3-7:
Cut away
fabric on right
side inside
stitched line.
Stabilizer
remains.

are doing, use an open-toed
or clear plastic appliqué foot.

- The easiest method for
  stitching the drawn lines is to
  lower or cover the feed dogs
  and to attach a circular embroidery or darning foot. Your
  hands then act as feed dogs
  and will guide the fabric
  through the machine. This
  method eliminates the te-
  diousness of constantly lifting
  the presser foot and turning
  the fabric.

- Remember to return the feed
  dogs to the original raised
  position when finished.

- Remove the circular embroidery foot and replace it with
  an appliqué foot (open-toed or
  clear plastic).

Fig. 3-8:
Zigzag over
straight stitch
with metallic
thread.

4. Next, on the fabric only, not
   the tear-away, cut away the
   center of the circle next to the
   machine stitching (Fig. 3-7).
   Do not remove the tear-off
   stabilizer.

5. Cover the straight stitches
   with a machine-sewn satin
   stitch (Fig. 3-8).

6. When all the shisha holes are
   covered, you have two
   choices to complete the
   shisha mirror insertion:

Fig. 3-9:
Machine
embroider
starburst
design around
machine
appliquéd
edge. Tear off
remaining
stabilizer.

- The traditional method is to
  machine embroider the area
  outside the satin stitches.
  Return the sewing machine to
  a covered or dropped feed
  dog position and replace the
  circular embroidery foot.
  With a straight stitch, machine embroider a starburst
  around the opening (Fig. 3-9).
  Be sure that this area is
  embroidered heavily enough
  to cover the original center
  satin stitches.

- The second method is to forego the outside machine embroidery and only use the original satin stitches. Tear off excess stabilizer.

7. Sandwich the mirror behind the opening with a scrap of woven fabric such as muslin. The woven fabric will not show on the front.

8. With the mirror centered behind the opening, pin all layers outside the satin stitches to hold all the parts in place.

9. With the sewing machine still set with the feed dogs down, the circular embroidery foot in place, and a straight-stitch mode, carefully straight stitch the layers together just outside the mirror's outside edge and around the outside edges of the satin stitches (Fig. 3-10). This can be done by turning the handwheel by hand. Work carefully, one stitch at a time, around the entire outside edge. If the needle comes in contact with the mirror's edge, the needle will break.

Fig. 3-10: Sandwich mirror in between the embroidered front opening and a new fabric backing and straight stitch around outside edge of satin stitch to hold in place.

10. The excess muslin can be trimmed off from behind the fabric at this time, if desired.

As explained previously, you must apply shisha mirrors to the fabrics before the whole project is completed. If the mirrors are to be used as embellishment on an appliquéd section, do it before the piece is appliquéd. If the background is to have shisha mirrors, do it before the project is quilted or constructed.

Shisha mirrors add glitz and shimmer, but they also add weight, especially the new mirrors. They also reflect sunlight and strong indoor lights. Before adding them to your patchwork piece, consider the garment's function, how often it will be worn, and the care you want to give it.

BUTTONS BY MACHINE

Adding buttons can dress up a garment with textural embellishment. On quilts, buttons also serve a functional purpose. If you substitute buttons for tacking or ties, they will hold your fabric layers together, while adding visual and textural design to your quilt.

Many people like to use antique buttons on garments or quilts (Fig. 3-11). Some of the jet black and glass buttons are wonderful when used in the right places. They may be found at antique shops, flea markets, and auctions. Button collectors have helped make the prices of these items seem unreasonable, but look at the price of some of the contemporary buttons for comparison.

You can sew on buttons with most sewing machines, as long as they are nonshank buttons with holes on the surface. The machine must be a zigzag sewing machine with an adjustable stitch width so it can be adjusted to the width between the holes in the button. If the sewing machine has only a limited number of adjustable widths, the left and right swing of the needle may not match the space between the two hole openings. Here's how:

1. Remove the sewing machine foot if you don't have a specific button sewing foot.

2. Try your darning or circular embroidery foot, but it may not have enough clearance between the bottom of the presser foot and the feed dogs for the button's depth.

3. The feed dogs need to be covered or dropped so that the button stays in place.

4. Stabilize the button temporarily with a fabric glue stick dabbed onto its back. You can also use double-faced tape to hold it in place. Or if you have long fingernails, hold the button in place just left of the sewing machine needle swing, safely out of the needle's way.

5. Lock threads at beginning and end by decentering the needle to the left or right, leaving the stitch width and length at 0, and stitching in one place several times.

Fig. 3-11: Antique jet black buttons and mother-of-pearl buttons.

6. Then, set the width to match the buttonholes.

7. The sewing machine needle should zigzag over the button about six times to hold it in place (Fig. 3-12).

8. A small dab of liquid sealant can be carefully dabbed onto the back (wrong) side of the threads to assure stability during wear.

Note: Use the same technique to tie a quilted area, either on the front or back of the quilt. You can use heavy yarn or 1/8" polyester satin ribbon for the ties. Tack the center by machine, then tie the yarn or ribbon in a bow or square knot.

Fig. 3-12: Button being sewn on by machine with no foot. Presser bar lever should be in the down position to engage upper thread tension.

SEW-ON JEWELS

You can buy both acrylic and Austrian crystal sew-on jewels. For obvious reasons, the acrylic jewels are much more affordable. They have a lot of shine and shimmer, but are not as shiny as the glass or crystal ones; however, they are a fraction of the cost of the cut crystal ones. Both jewels can be machine-washed, but turn the garment inside out.

Both of these types of jewels are easily sewn on with the sewing machine. Practice on the acrylic jewels, as they will not chip or shatter if they are accidentally hit by a sewing machine

needle. You need a zigzag sewing machine to machine stitch on these jewels.

1. Cover or lower the feed dogs and remove the presser foot.

2. Set the zigzag width to clear the distance between the hole and the outside edge of the sew-on jewel.

3. Hold the jewel in place with your left forefinger to the left of the needle.

4. The left swing of the needle goes into the hole opening and the right swing of the needle goes to the right edge of the jewel onto the background. If there is a hole on another part of the jewel, the project can be turned around to sew down the other side.

5. Secure the threads by dabbing the back (wrong) side with liquid sealant.

Large beads can be sewn onto a project in this same manner. The thread will show more so it should be the same color as the bead. Rayon or metallic threads would be good choices.

Use the same method for metallic or plastic bangles. If the piece to be sewn on is silver, use silver metallic thread, so the sewing will not be seen as prominently.

BEADS

INDIVIDUAL BEADS

Individual beads can be sewn on by machine, but the process is tedious. Here's how:

1. Use a smaller needle (#65-70/9-10) that will slide through the entire bead.

2. Slide the bead the length of the thinner part of the needle to be sure that the bead will not break apart. If the needle is too fat, the bead will either split or will not sew onto the project. Remove the bead.

3. Lower or cover the feed dogs and remove the foot.

4. To lock the stitches before sewing the beads, sew several stitches in place, with no bead.

5. Next, place a bead onto the tip of the needle, sliding upwards through the hole of the bead.

6. Take a stitch through the hole, then one outside the bead. This secures the bead onto the background.

7. Repeat each stitch series for each bead.

8. Secure the stitches by locking your stitch at the end. To do this, stitch in place several times.

9. Place a clear sealant on the back to secure thread ends.

BY–THE–YARD BEADS

By-the-yard beads, such as faux pearls (plastic beads) and real crystal beads (slung beads) are available for purchase and can all be sewn on by machine (Figs. 3-13, 3-14).

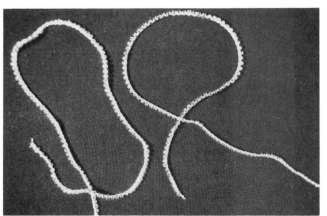

Fig. 3-13: Clutch with beads-by-the-yard and buttons as embellishments.

It is best to start stitching the beads at an outside raw edge and to finish at an outside raw edge. If the carrying thread ravels, dab the beads on these cut edges with a clear sealant, and if the end of the beads will not be sewn into a seam allowance, use the clear sealant first on the raw edge to be left exposed and let it air-dry. Afterwards, sew it onto the surface as desired. The sealed-off edge will hold the beads in place on the cut-off edge.

The easiest method for sewing on beads-by-the-yard is to zigzag over them (Fig. 3-15). Some machines have sewing machine feet with a tunnel underneath (e.g., Bernina's bulky overlock foot) that will allow the beads to pass under-

neath (see Source List). If your machine does not have this type of foot, you can sometimes use a circular embroidery foot. If the beads do not clear underneath easily, the presser foot can be lifted slightly, every few stitches, to ease it along. They can also be sewn on with no foot, but some

Fig. 3-14: Glass beads by the yard.

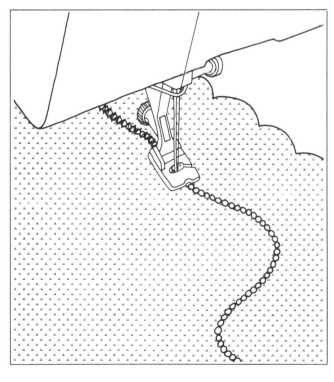

sewing machines will not catch the upper and lower threads without any foot. Don't let the

Fig. 3-15: Beads being sewn on with a bulky overlock foot.

fabric lift from the needle plate or stitches will be skipped. Press your fingers firmly against the fabric on either side of the needle.

When sewing on the beads, be sure that your sewing machine has a zigzag wide enough to clear the beads right and left. The stitch length should be 3.0 or 8–10 stitches to the inch. The feed dogs should be in an uncovered, up position. The best thread to use is invisible or clear thread on the top and regular thread matching the background in the bobbin.

When the outside raw edges containing bead lengths are to be sewn into a seam allowance,

they have to be sewn across carefully:

1. Pin together the seam allowances.

2. Mark the position of the beads in the seam allowance with pins on each side of them.

3. When the sewing machine sews to a pin, stop. Carefully turn the hand wheel to sew across the beaded area so that the machine catches all the layers without breaking the beads. This method will also work on a serger by carefully turning the hand wheel over the beads instead of using the foot pedal.

PIPED-EDGE PEARLS AND BEADS

Pearls and beads may be purchased already attached to the edge of tape—usually twill tape (Fig. 3-16). They resemble piping and are sewn in the same manner. (See page 114 on bias tape.) This beaded trim needs to be sewn into a seam allowance with a zipper foot. The ends of the carrying thread should be sealed off with a clear sealant. When these trims are to be sewn into a seam allowance, use the

method for by-the-yard beads as explained in the previous paragraphs.

Fig. 3-16: Pearls on twill tape.

SEQUINS-BY-THE-YARD

The earliest sequins available for purchase by the yard were made from soft metal paillettes. Contemporary sequins-by-the-yard are made from soft plastic. Both types of sequins are made by putting metallic colors onto the surface of the paillettes. The sequins are strung together with a chain stitch of thread. When the sequin yardage is cut, the chain stitches will unravel slightly. The cut edges of the thread should be dabbed with a clear sealant to keep them from raveling further.

An easy method for stitching on sequins-by-the-yard is to machine zigzag over them, as follows (Fig. 3-17).

1. Set the sewing machine at a wide enough zigzag to clear both the right and left edges of the sequins. Many of the older sewing machines do not swing wide enough to clear the sequin edges. Therefore, the needle will pierce the sequins frequently. This is not a problem for either metallic or plastic sequins. When the needle pierces the sequins, they will not break or split, nor will the needle. Newer sewing machines have a wider swing and will present no problem with clearing the edges.

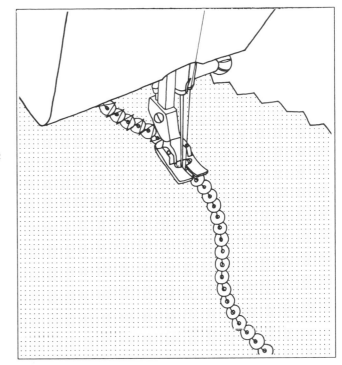

2. Thread the machine with clear plastic thread on the top and matching background regular sewing thread on the bobbin.

3. It is easiest to use an open-toed or clear plastic appliqué foot to zigzag over the sequins.

4. Determine the sewing direction so that the presser foot runs down the smooth side, reducing friction. The sequins have a snakeskin-like texture. If you run your fingers on them in one direction, they lie smooth. In the other direction, they are rough and the edges catch. If the machine runs down the rough side, the presser foot will catch onto

Fig. 3-17: Sequins-by-the-yard being sewn on by machine with an appliqué foot.

the sequin edge and possibly bend it. You would also have to raise the foot frequently to ease the sequins through. If the sequins are going through on the smooth side, there is no problem with catching.

Another method of applying sequins is to put a #90/14 needle in the sewing machine. Thread the machine in a thread color to match the sequins or a clear plastic thread. Then topstitch sequins in place with a straight stitch piercing the sequins. This technique can be used to cover the edges of a fused appliqué replacing satin stitches over the raw edges.

There are three new generic presser feet available from Clotilde which will facilitate sewing on beads, sequins, trims, and ribbons (see Source List).

LARGE PAILLETTES

These large individual sequins are manufactured like the smaller ones. They are made with either a small or large hole on one side. The larger paillettes are popular embellishments easily added to knitted projects. The paillettes can be slid onto a knitting needle with each additional stitch, to result in a glitzy sweater.

These sequins can also be sewn on in layers on a sewing machine. You can make a thick, fishscale-like texture by sewing on each sequin with a zigzag stitch (Fig. 3-18). The left swing of the needle should sew through the hole, while the right swing should clear the right edge onto the background.

1. Since the surface of the paillettes is large, smooth, and shiny, any marks show easily. A Teflon foot would slide across these sequins easily, but other presser feet rub against the sequin edges and leave a mark. Therefore, cover or lower the feed dogs and use a darning or circular embroidery foot.

Fig. 3-18:
Large cluster of paillettes on fish coat.

2. Attach the sequins in rows starting at the bottom of the section and moving upwards by rows to the final row on the top.

3. If the project is to be pressed with an iron, it should be done lightly on the wrong side, or not at all. Any heat, whether dry or steam, will dull the color of the sequin and could ultimately melt the plastic.

RATTAIL CORDING

Satin spaghetti cording, commonly called rattail cord, is a slippery, shiny cord that comes in many vibrant colors. It can be decoratively machine-sewn down to a surface.

Set your machine with the feed dogs up, uncovered, and attach a presser foot with a tunnel underneath the center of the foot (embroidery or bulky overlock). The cord will tunnel underneath the foot. A darning, circular embroidery, or large pin-tuck foot will also work adequately. Thread the machine with a matching color rayon or a clear plastic thread.

Use a 3.0 or 8–10 stitch length. The zigzag width should clear the cord so the stitch crisscrosses over the cord as it is sewn in place (Fig. 3-19). The raw edges of the cord should be on the outside raw edges or underneath another (wider) edge of an appliqué or trim.

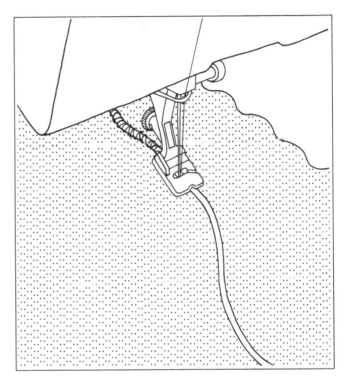

Fig. 3-19: Rattail being sewn with a bulky overlock foot.

Rattail cording can be looped or buried underneath another edge—for example, to make the stamens in the center of flowers. You can make your own rattail by sewing narrow strips of fabric into a tube and turning them right sides out. Tools like FastTurn make this easy.

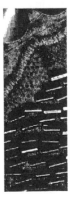

BIAS TRIMS

Using bias trims decoratively is an artistic and fun way to embellish garments and quilts. It is inexpensive, especially if the bias is self-made, and it is easy to apply by machine.

Bias tape is available packaged in a large selection of colors. These tapes are made from poly-cotton fabrics and therefore will not shrink or fade with laundering. They do save time, since no preparation is involved in making them. There are several choices of sizes: 1/2"-wide single fold, 1"-wide single fold, and 1/2"-wide double fold. A single-fold bias tape is originally cut 1" wide and the edges are turned under 1/4" on each side to create a finished 1/2" single-fold bias tape. The double-fold 1/2"-inch bias tape is cut 1-1/2" wide and the outside edges are turned under 1/4" on each side. The entire 1" finished bias tape is then folded in half to make a finished 1/2" double-folded tape. This tape now has four layers of fabric and can be used on an outside raw edge of a fabric project to bind off both the top and the underneath edge at the same time. One edge is slightly smaller so that the double-fold tape can be top-stitched over the outside raw edges in one step to catch both sides. The larger fold should be on the underneath side.

The double-folded tape can be used as surface decoration, such as folded back on itself to form geometric patterns. The disadvantage of using this double-fold bias is that it is much thicker. The advantage of using all-bias strips is that they will curve in the design because they are cut on the stretchy bias of the fabric. Ribbons cannot be used in the same way because they are woven on the straight of grain and will not curve.

If you want to match your bias colors to fabrics used in your patchwork, you will probably have to make your own bias tape. Knowing how to make bias tape will allow you to use tapes of any color and any width. Not only that, self-made bias tape is less expensive than purchased tape. It does take some time to prepare.

As you know, the bias is the diagonal weave of the fabric. The lengthwise threads have absolutely no stretch to them and the crosswise threads have only a little bit of stretch. The bias has a great deal of stretch. If you pull on the diagonal of your fabric, you will be able to tell the bias of the fabric immediately (Fig. 3-20). This stretching capability is disastrous when used improperly in a garment. However, it is an absolute necessity when this stretch is needed. The stretching qualities are important for curves around the outside of shapes or curved designs on appliquéd projects.

Fig. 3-21: Bias tape maker and bias bars in use.

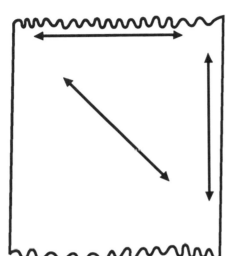

Fig. 3-20: The true bias is shown as the diagonal line on the drawing.

MAKING BIAS TAPE

You can make bias tapes several ways. The simplest method is to cut bias strips with a rotary cutter and run them through a gadget called a bias tape maker, which comes in different sizes and is available in shops and by mail order. Bias tape makers are made of metal and are tapered at one end (Fig. 3-21). A thin metal handle moves upward so that the bias tape maker can be grasped and pulled along as you iron the tape leaving the tool.

1. Cut the fabric strips 1/2" larger than the desired finished width. For example, a 1" finished bias strip should be cut 1-1/2".

2. When cutting the bias strips, stack them up with all the right sides of the fabric upwards.

3. Then cut the short ends at a 45-degree angle. It's easiest to cut off the ends with a rotary cutter and a plastic 45-degree miter marker.

4. To join bias strips, place the short ends with right sides together. Strips should form an upside-down "V" (Fig. 3-22).

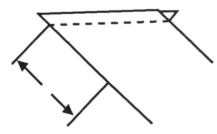

5. Sew across with a 1/4" seam.

Fig. 3-22: Join bias strips as shown.

6. Press seam open and trim points of seams even with edge of bias strip. (Fig. 3-23). The strip is now ready to be ironed through the bias tape maker.

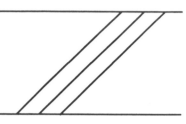

Fig. 3-23: Press seam open.

7. Feed one end through the wide end of the bias tape maker. It will exit the narrow end with the edges turned under 1/4" on each side. If the fabric exiting the bias tape maker is ironed with the turned-under edges upward, the iron can press the edges unevenly, particularly at seam lines.

8. Hold the metal bar with one hand.

9. Hold the preheated steam iron on the exit side of the bias tape maker and press against the tape maker.

10. Tilt the tape maker slightly upwards and slowly move it along the length of the ironing board, feeding the cut bias through as you go. With the other hand, slide the iron against the moving tape maker.

11. Roll the ironed-under or finished bias tape onto a cardboard tube or other cylindrical container. (If you are a recycler, paper-towel tubes are perfect for this purpose.)

12. Use masking tape to secure the first edge to the roll and continue rolling the bias tape onto the roll until all the bias is ironed. If you do not roll up the tape as it is made, the newly pressed-under edges do not always remain pressed flat. The roll will keep the finished tape flat and neat, and it is easy to use in a project as it comes off the roll.

13. Secure the final end onto the roll with a straight pin.

The one type of fabric that should be handled differently is sheer fabric, such as thin China or ribbon silk. When it is pressed as it comes out of the bias tape maker, it shrinks. A remedy is to cut these fabrics in strips 1/4" wider than the specified finished width (including 1/2" extra for turn under on edges). When the fabric shrinks with the steam heat from the iron, it will finish to the proper size.

If you don't have a bias tape maker, you can turn under and press the edges manually. This is not only inaccurate but it is dangerous to the fingers. You will not get a consistent width throughout your tape; and you probably will have burned fingers.

A different way to make bias trim is to use metal strips of different widths, called Celtic Bar Makers. These are available by mail order and in quilt shops. Here's how:

1. Cut your strips 1/2" wider than the finished bar size and seam the short ends together as described in the previous section to make one long strip.

2. Fold the strips in half the long way, wrong sides together, and sew with a 1/4" seam allowance. Some sewing machines have feed dogs that do not push a narrow seam allowance through properly. If you need to sew larger than 1/4" seam allowances, cut a wider strip and sew a larger seam allowance. Then trim the seam allowances to 1/4" or less.

3. After the entire strip is seamed, insert a Celtic bar maker into one end.

4. Hide the raw edges of the seam allowances underneath the pressed strip, with both seam allowances pressed to one side.

5. Press over the metal strip.

6. The finished ironed strip can also be rolled onto a tube for later use as explained previously.

This technique allows bias strips to be made in small sizes; therefore trimming very thin seam allowances is sometimes necessary.

If you need very thin strips for vines or stems, you will not be able to use the methods explained above. For these thin strips:

1. Cut your bias strips 1/2" wide.

2. Fold and stitch the strips as before, using a 1/8" seam allowance.

3. After the strips are seamed and trimmed, they can be pressed flat, with raw edges underneath. Do not use a metal bar.

4. Because the seam is as wide as the finished strip, this must be done very carefully. You may want to trim the seam allowances even smaller.

Another method of making bias stems does not require that the bias be folded before application.

1. Cut the strips four times the desired width of the finished strip. (For a finished strip 1/8" wide, cut the strip 1/2" wide.)

2. Fold the strips in half with wrong sides together and iron as before.

3. Place the strip on the section of fabric where it will be needed and sew directly onto the background using a 1/8" seam.

4. When you have stitched the entire length, press the bias over to cover the seam and it is ready to stitch down as desired. This method makes it possible to have very narrow strips such as those that might be used on floral stems. Remember that if you are using a decorative stitch or appliqué stitch by machine to hold the bias strips down, you must make the first stitched side (the one you sewed before folding the tape over itself) appear to be attached the same as the other side, so you must restitch along that side as well.

Some sewers consider the following method of making a continuous strip of bias tape faster and easier, while others find it takes more time to figure out the cutting dimensions required for the procedure than it takes to cut the strips and sew them together as explained above. This is a personal preference.

To make continuous bias strips, use a square piece of cloth. The size depends on how much and how big a piece of binding you need. A 36" square yields approximately 20 yards of 1-3/4" to 2-1/4"-wide bias strips. Use that size as a basis for other yardage amounts as required.

1. Cut the square in half along the diagonal (Fig. 3-24).

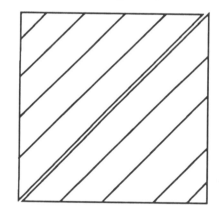

Fig. 3-24: Cut square in half along the diagonal.

2. Join the two resulting pieces together along the straight sides to form a parallelogram, using a 1/4" seam allowance (Fig. 3-25).

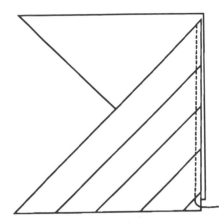

*Fig. 3-25:
Join the two
pieces to form
a parallel-
ogram.*

3. Using a pencil or a water-
erasable marker, mark lines
1–3/4" (or any other width
desired for finished bias;
Fig. 3-26).

*Fig. 3-26:
Mark lines at
desired width.*

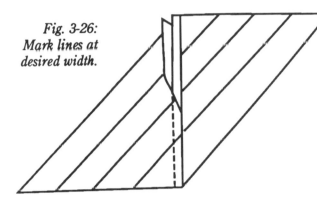

4. If there is a remainder on
the last edge less than the
width desired, trim it away.

5. Sew the parallelogram
together to form a tube,
matching your first drawn
line to your second drawn
line on the opposite side
(Fig. 3-27).

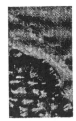

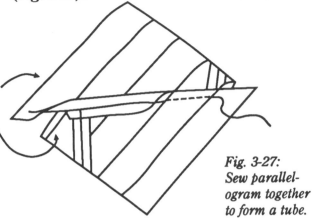

*Fig. 3-27:
Sew parallel-
ogram together
to form a tube.*

6. After stitching, cut along
your marked lines to result
in one long continuous bias
strip (Fig. 3-28). This
method saves time in cut-
ting individual strips and in
sewing shorter sections
together.

*Fig. 3-28:
Cut along lines
to form one
continuous
strip.*

SEWING BIAS STRIPS

Your bias strips, whether made or purchased, can be topstitched to the project with the sewing machine, but it is not very attractive and it has less give on the stitched curves. They can also be hand stitched, as in hand appliqué. The look of hand appliqué can be achieved by machine using the blind hem stitch (Fig. 3-29). This same stitch is used to machine stitch hems in garments so they cannot be easily seen when the garment is finished.

1. Thread the upper part of the machine with clear invisible thread, so it will not show when stitched.

2. Thread the bobbin with regular sewing thread in a color to match the background fabric.

3. For easier visibility, use an open-toed or appliqué foot.

4. Set your machine on blind hem stitch.

5. Set stitch length at 1.5 and stitch width at 1.5. Some new computer machines cannot set the stitch length and width at this low setting. They are preprogrammed to be set only between certain number settings. However, the turnover or mirror stitch button will have a different set of number capabilities. Sometimes the mirrored

stitch will accommodate the lower number settings and the regular setting will not.

6. Experiment on a scrap to see if your settings will stitch an invisible-looking blind hem stitch. The "V" of the swing should both catch the edge of the bias and be narrow enough so that the actual "V" is not opened up much. The off-the-edge straight stitches should be close together, just off the edge of the bias strip. Clear thread will help to camouflage the stitches. The blind hem stitch looks like the stitches in hand appliqué. Some sewing machines, particularly some Elnas, do not have the little straight stitches between the "V" swing of the needle and the next "V" swing. Instead, they stitch in a slight zigzag. This type of stitch will also be acceptable for blind hem appliqué.

Fig. 3-29: Finished vest uses lamé bias strips sewn with blind hem stitch on vines.

7. When the bias is pinned onto the background fabric, it may have several curves in the design. If there are hard curves in the design, the inside curved edge of the bias should be stitched first. The outside edge should be stitched last.

8. If several bias strips are to be pinned and stitched next to each other, start at one outside edge and blind

hemstitch each edge of the bias strips until all the edges are stitched.

9. Raw outside edges are to be turned under or placed under other bias strips or appliqué motifs. Fig. 3-30 shows how to butt ends.

Fig. 3-30: Butting edges of bias binding at beginning and end.

THREE-DIMENSIONAL APPLIQUÉ

Free-form and three-dimensional appliqué techniques provide another way to embellish your project (Fig. 3-31).

The easiest method to sew a motif is to find an existing printed motif in fabric yardage. There are endless selections of these. Flowers and leaves can be cut out of home decorating fabrics—particularly cotton chintz prints. These prints usually have a rich selection of colors and resemble antique chintzes that were used in

broderie perse quilts. These quilts were made by cutting out floral motifs, and then appliquéing them to a background fabric. They were elaborate, with many different cut-out designs on one quilt.

If you want to achieve a more contemporary look or a juvenile theme, modern prints, such as jungle cats and kid's fabrics, can also be used.

When using a purchased fabric for a motif, choose a

Fig. 3-31: Belt shown uses three-dimensional appliqué.

fabric that has the motifs separated from each other rather than overlapped. It is hard to use a jungle cat whose legs are partially hidden underneath a foliage motif (Fig. 3-32).

When choosing the matching thread, consider whether the thread should be the same color as the background that it will be stitched onto, or the color of the background of the motif. If the latter, it will blend into the motif. If, however, a new color is introduced altogether, this will set off the motif from both the motif and the background. A metallic thread can be used to give it some pizzazz if desired. (See Chapter 1 on threads.)

1. Cut out the motifs at least 1/4" apart from each other, but 1" is better.

2. Then back the cut-out motif with both a scrap of batting and a lining or backing fabric.

3. Hold these three layers together with a straight pin in the center of the motif.

4. To stitch this appliqué section, set the sewing machine at a regular straight stitch. Begin stitching around the motif 1/8" outside the edge of the design (Fig. 3-33). Remember that the piece will later be satin-stitched over and the swing of the needle should stop just short of the edge of the

Fig. 3-33: Sandwich batting between top fabric motif and backing piece. Straight stitch around outside of motif and cut away all layers close to stitching. Fabric from Concord House.

Fig. 3-34: Satin stitch all around motif to finish edges. Fabric from Beacon Hill Collection from Concord House.

motif. This is why you need to stitch 1/8" beyond the edge of the motif and not on the outside edge of the motif.

5. After straight-stitching the three layers, cut away the excess top fabric, batting and lining from outside the straight-stitched edge.

6. Set the sewing machine on a medium satin stitch (Fig. 3-34). (When the raw outside edge is satin stitched over, the stitches will appear narrower than a regular appliqué satin stitch.)

7. Use an open-toed or clear plastic appliqué foot for best visibility.

8. The feed dogs on some machines do not move along the fabric easily. If your sewing machine has

difficulty satin stitching over an edge, simply place the appliqué piece on a piece of tissue paper, thin typing paper, or water-soluble stabilizer. Stitch through all the layers with the paper sandwiched between the appliqué piece and the feed dogs. The paper will tear off easily after stitching. (If a tear-off stabilizer is used, it will get sewn into the stitches and some of the remaining white tear-off paper product will remain. This will not happen with paper. However, when stitching onto regular paper, the needle will dull quickly and will need changing more frequently.)

9. When you come to an outside or inside point, lift the presser foot to turn the motif. The left swing of the

needle on the satin stitch should remain down in the fabric before the presser foot is lifted. This will keep the appliqué piece from slipping.

10. If the satin-stitched edges do not cover the raw edges enough, satin stitch around the entire motif a second time. If the satin stitches are too close and the machine is not moving over the stitches easily, loosen the stitch length of the stitches slightly.

When the three-dimensional pieces are finished on the outside, they can be machine quilted on the interior. When larger motifs are used, machine quilting is helpful to hold the layers together, and it adds texture. If metallic threads are used, they highlight the entire motif. The machine quilting should be done with straight stitches, either freeform or with the presser foot down. If the pieces are hard to handle and turn, place them on a piece of paper or tear-off stabilizer underneath to facilitate the machine quilting.

Make several of these threedimensional appliqué pieces so that you can arrange them artistically. If you are decorating a small section of a project, such as a belt or the shoulder of a vest or blouse, stitch at least five to seven pieces. To decorate a quilt or a large section of a garment, you will need many such motifs.

The project to be decorated should be laid out flat on a flat surface. Then arrange the threedimensional pieces in the appropriate section. They can be layered, with edges of some pieces underneath others. Pin each of these pieces in place with long, straight pins.

When the project is ready to be stitched in place, return the machine to a regular straight stitch and use a larger #90/14 needle. The thread should be the same color as the satin stitches. If you used a lot of different thread colors for the satin stitching, use invisible thread so that you don't need to constantly change the thread colors. Use an open-toed or clear plastic appliqué foot for best visibility.

1. Straight stitch the pieces onto the background next to the inside edge of the satin stitches.

2. Stitch the layered pieces first.

3. Stitch them in place in short segments on at least two opposite sides to hold them in place. Do not stitch around the entire piece, as the continuous stitching holds the pieces too flat and takes away from the three-dimensional effect. This technique allows the appliqué shapes to extend beyond the outside edge of the project and gives you more freedom to decorate the project.

Small, thin bias strips of fabric can be blind-hem appliquéd onto the background if desired. (See bias tape section earlier in this chapter.) These can be used as vines and stems on the flower and leaf motifs. Refer to Fig. 3-29.

You can use the same technique on hand-drawn shapes transferred to fabric. Synthetic suede scraps, too, can be made into three-dimensional appliqué with this method. Although the cut edges of the synthetic suede do not ravel, a narrow, dense satin stitch on the outside edge gives the fabric a finished look. The fabric will not break apart, unlike natural leathers and suedes; the close stitching would break off the outside edges of the skins at the stitching line.

Satin stitch synthetic suede in one layer only, with no batting or backing. If you're making a flower with synthetic suede:

1. Fold some of the flower petals over the center.

2. Then insert center stamens into the fold, using either looped rattail (see page 113) or imitation stamens (purchased at a craft or floral supply store).

3. Catch them into the stitching for a more realistic and three-dimensional flower.

4. Machine embroider the outside leaves with veins, using a darker shade of thread, before placing them underneath the flowers.

RIBBONS AND STRAIGHT-GRAIN WOVEN TRIMS

Ribbons and trims are made using a variety of fabrics, threads and widths. They provide another method of adding surface design to glitz up a project. Metallic woven ribbons are more dramatic than satin ribbons. Grosgrain ribbon is ridged on the surface and does not have as much shine as the satin and metallic ribbons.

Ribbons are woven on the straight of grain. This means that they do not easily curve

and bend as bias-grain trims do. This is also the case with woven trims. One of the other problems with these trims is that the cut edges ravel. When decorating a project, it is important that the unfinished edges are either covered up, turned under, or sewn into the seam allowances.

When the ribbons and trims are to be topstitched onto a project, they must be held in place for stitching, but satin ribbons tend to retain pin

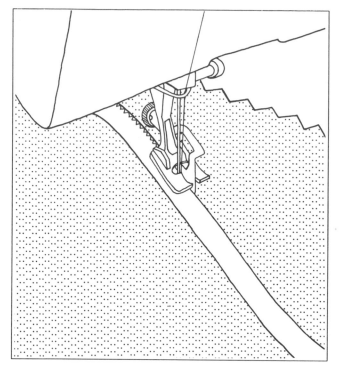

Fig. 3-35: Ribbon being sewn on using an edge foot.

straight and even. Some machines have a foot with a tempered metal band in the center. Move the needle position over to the left side of the metal strip. As the ribbon feeds into the foot, the metal band acts as a guide to hold the ribbon next to it (Fig. 3-35). The needle stitches neatly along the edge of the ribbon. Stitch on each side of the ribbon in the same direction, if possible. This keeps the ribbon flat, with no puckers as it is stitched.

If ribbons are loosely twisted and draped over the surface, tack them in place to hold them secure. If tacked with a button or a bead, you can sew them on with a sewing machine. (See pages 106 and 108 on embellishments.) But if no embellishments are used, bar-tack the ribbon with the sewing machine. Lower or cover the feed dogs and set the machine on a zigzag stitch. Thread the machine with matching thread, such as rayon, and put an appliqué foot on the machine. Simply run the machine about six stitches in place to hold the ribbon.

Silk ribbon is available in narrow widths. It is very soft and pliable. Unlike synthetic ribbons, it can be twisted and draped onto the project and topstitched in place continuously.

holes. You need not pin ribbons that are trimming an edge of a project. Instead hold them down as you sew, eyeballing the line as you go. If you are not sure of your stitching, use a silver pencil (Berol is the best brand to use) and lightly draw a line on one of the stitching edges which the ribbon will later cover. Topstitch just over the drawn line, holding the ribbon up in front of the foot so you can follow the line. If the cut ends of the ribbon are not sewn into the seam allowance, turn under the ends of the cut ribbon so that no raw edges show.

Straight stitch or zigzag the ribbon with a matching thread. It is sometimes hard to keep the needle exactly straight on the outside edge of the ribbon and keep the ribbon edge

WEAVING RIBBONS

Ribbons can be woven together and used as a pillow top, accessory, or garment section. The easiest method for weaving ribbons is to find an appropriate size of Foam Core or heavy cardboard.

1. Cover one side of the board with a piece of fusible interfacing, glue side up. If the woven piece is to be machine appliquéd, place a paper-backed fusible webbing on the board, rough side up.

2. Pin half of the ribbons along one edge of the board. Be sure to pin the ribbons inside the fusible product's edge.

3. Weave the other ribbons through the pinned ribbons. As you are weaving the ribbons, be sure that they are butted against each other, edge to edge. There should be no spaces between the ribbons.

4. After all the ribbons are woven carefully together, unpin each outside edge around the entire edge and repin the ribbons onto the underneath fusible product.

5. Cover the piece with stiff fabric or paper to help flip it over.

6. Flip the woven piece onto an ironing board, or if the piece is too large, use a flat board covered with a clean towel.

7. Carefully iron on the back of the fusible product, from the center outwards. Do not push or pull the iron. Lift it when moving it to a new section. Sliding the iron may move the woven ribbons out of place.

8. Remove the outside pins before the iron presses them. The finished, fused section is now a new, woven, original piece of fabric which can be cut out and sewn into the project.

If the woven piece is fused onto paper fusible webbing instead of fusible interfacing, the desired shapes can be drawn onto the paper, cut out, and machine appliquéd in place. Use rayon or metallic threads that match the ribbon colors. (Refer to page 18 on thread.)

Ribbon can also be cut out and sewn into patchwork as if it were fabric. This is a good solution when you want to add a touch of velvet, moiré, lamé, or satin to a project. Since 1/4" seam allowances will be sewn on each side, purchase the ribbon 1/2" wider than the desired finished width of your patchwork strip. Using ribbons in patchwork will be more

economical than purchasing fabric yardages, unless the whole project is made with ribbons. You may also find a larger selection of colors and textures. Ribbons are also used in contemporary tied quilts, the tying being done with thin, 1/8" polyester satin ribbon. The ties go through the fabric top, batting, and backing of the quilt. Sometimes the tying is done on the top of the quilt, while other quilts are tied from the back.

Other straight-grain woven trims are available for use on patchwork projects. Gold and silver rickrack trims can be incorporated to glitz up Seminole patchwork. Simply topstitch the rickrack in place with a matching metallic thread. You can twist and turn the rickrack trims or sew them perfectly straight. The metallic colors will give the project a contemporary look.

PIPING

Piping is fabric-covered cording. It turns a common-place project into something smashing. If piping is used throughout a piece, it adds a texture that cannot be reproduced by any other method (Fig. 3-36).

As a finish on furniture, it prevents wear and tear on seams and makes the piece more durable. On garments, it can perform that same function, but adds detail that separates designer fashions from off-the-rack. On quilts, piping has not yet been used to its fullest potential, perhaps because fabric cording sewn on by hand is tedious to apply. But we sewing-machine lovers know how to apply it by machine. Only thin cording can be sewn on this way. You need a sewing-machine foot with a large tunnel opening underneath (cording or bulky overlock foot)

which allows you to loosely zigzag over the cording. Later in this chapter we'll explain how. As you will learn, you can create many wonderful things with piping.

Fig. 3-36: Silver piping inserted in patchwork on bodice of dress.

Piping can be purchased ready to use or you can make it yourself from a variety of fabrics. If you can't find premade piping in your local sewing store, shop in upholstery stores. For example, you can now buy piping made from lamé fabrics. To add a subtle shimmer to your garment, use lamé piping with no lamé in the background.

Piping is also available in a wide range of sizes, up to 1" thick. This size is used mostly for decorating projects and is not suitable for use in clothing. It is both heavy in weight and inflexible to work with. Use it on long seams and on outside edges.

Very narrow piping has a wide range of uses in surface decoration: outlining the center of a medallion quilt, accenting seams in the borders of patchwork, defining the edge of an appliquéd design, and more.

MAKING YOUR OWN PIPING

You can inexpensively purchase the cording used as filler in piping in a variety of thicknesses, made of soft cotton or a stiffer polyester. Its availability may determine your choice.

1. Cover the cording with bias tape or bias strips. (See pages 115–116 on bias tape for instructions on cutting bias.)

Bias is used because it has the most stretch and will conform to curving shapes. The width of the cording determines the width to cut the fabric bias strips. Cut them twice the width of the cording plus twice the seam allowances. For garments with 5/8" seam allowances add 1-1/4". For 1/4" patchwork seam allowances, add 1/2". For example, if you are using 1/4" cording, and you are making a jacket, cut your bias strips 1-3/4" wide. If you are making piping insertion for a quilt, cut the strips 1" wide.

If you are using lamé as the fabric covering for your piping, use either tissue lamé or tricot lamé. (See pages 87 and 92.) If using tissue lamé, you don't need a fusible underneath to prevent fraying because lamé cut on the bias will not fray. If using tricot-backed lamé, remember that the backing will add a little extra bulk and that if placed in sections where hard wear is expected, the metallic finish might wear off.

2. Seam the strips of bias material together as described in the section on bias tape (page 115).

3. Fold the raw edges over the cord so that the two edges are even, cording against the wrong sides of the fabric.

4. Set the sewing machine on a regular straight stitch, using a zipper foot instead of the usual presser foot. The zipper foot allows the needle to stitch close to, but not through, the cording. Some zipper feet have the ability to move from one side of the needle to the other, while the needle remains stationary. Other machines have a stationary zipper foot and the needle is moved instead.

5. If you are making a lot of piping and have purchased a reel of cording to work from, cut off the appropriate piping cord length before sewing. If left on the reel while adding the fabric covering, the cording will twist as it is pulled off the reel and the fabric folded over the cord will begin to twist as well. If the cording is cut off and left free, it can be straightened out as you sew. Set the stitch length on 3.0 or 8-10 stitches to the inch to reduce any puckering. A tighter stitch will not make smooth, finished piping. Purchased piping is stitched with a commercial machine that makes a straight chain stitch. Use a thread that will match closely the color of the bias fabric strips. On a fabric such as gold lamé, use a yellow matching general

thread in both the top and bobbin. When covering the cording with the bias strips, keep the needle as close to the edge of the covered cord as possible.

If the bias fabric used as a covering is slippery or difficult to sew, especially on narrow cording, another method will make sewing trouble-free. If your machine has a foot with a large tunnel underneath (cording or bulky overlock foot), the piping can be fed underneath the foot with the raw edges to one side. The needle position is then moved over toward the raw edges. As the piping feeds through the foot, it will come out sewn into perfect piping.

APPLYING PIPING

If the outside edges of a sewing project are to be piped, pin the raw edges of the piping toward the project's outside raw edges. The piping should lie toward the center of the project. If you are sewing a project with a seam allowance larger than the piping seam allowance, pin the piping further from the project's raw edges, so the two seam lines match.

MAKING A SQUARE CORNER

To go around an outside square corner, pin the piping near the corner. Then clip the piping's raw edges, stopping short of the turned corner and next to the sewn straight stitches next to the piping cord. The clipped edges should be clipped the same distance from the turned edge as the seam allowance used before you came to the corner. The clipped piping will turn at a perfect 90-degree angle and the corner turned will look like a square was cut out of the raw edges (Fig. 3-37).

Turning an inside corner is similar. The point where the piping turns is also clipped, but there will be an excess of fabric rather than an open section. It is best to cut a "V" out of the corner to eliminate the excess fabric.

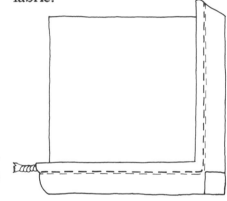

Fig. 3-37: Making a square corner.

When turning inside curves, cut narrow "V"s from the raw edges. This will help eliminate any extra bulk and will keep the piping flat. Clip outside curves.

It is easiest to straight stitch the pinned piping in place first before joining a second layer of fabric. Using this method will save ripping out the fabric later in case all the layers do not get caught in the seam allowances.

JOINING ENDS

There are two methods for joining the two ends of piping when they meet. The first:

1. Start sewing the piping about 1" from its cut-off edge. The total length of the piping should then be 1" longer than the original sewn edge.

2. Rip the stitches on the piping for that 1" and cut off the cord. Later both raw cord ends will butt end to end. Be sure not to cut off too much; this will leave a gap.

3. Fold under the fabric 1/4" and then wrap the entire folded-under fabric over the beginning edge of the piping.

4. Restitch the ripped-out stitches as you stitch the piping in place.

The other method is to carefully seam the two raw edges of fabric at a 45-degree angle.

1. First cut the cording so that both raw ends of the cords butt together.

2. Clip back the stitching on the piping on both ends.

3. Cut each of the two raw ends 1/4" longer than the finished seam.

4. Sew the two raw ends together with a 1/4" seam allowance.

5. Fold the new seam over the butted cording and resew the edges next to the cording (Fig. 3-38). This method, although a little more tedious, will make a perfect continuous piped edge.

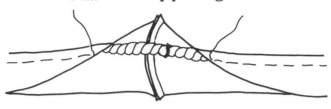

Fig. 3-38: Joining piping ends.

SECTIONAL PIPING

If an inside border is to be piped, use the same method as discussed for piped appliqué on page 136. The outside fabric edge will look like a facing that shows on the outside and is effective on both quilts or garments.

Sometimes the same effect can be achieved with a folded bias strip of fabric with no piping cord inside (Fig. 3-39). This will lie flat, but still set off the two sections of background fabric and give the project a bit of texture. You can cut strips on the straight grain if they do not turn corners. Simply determine the desired finished width of the strip, double that measurement, and add 1/2". Cut four strips, fold in half right sides out, and press. Pin to quilt or patchwork edge facing toward the project's center, matching edges, and stitch in place. Stitch opposite sides first, then ends. At corners, stitch strips on top of each other, not mitered.

You can easily cut apart and pipe sections of a garment in a curved, free-form method:

1. Use a medium-sized piping.

2. Cut a foundation of woven lining fabric for each pattern piece you will cut and pipe—e.g., the bodice. The foundation fabric should not be slippery or ravelly.

Fig. 3-39: This quilt uses folded fabric strips instead of piping to add a break between borders.

3. Cover the right edge of the foundation with a section of fabric and stay-stitch close to the outside edges.

4. Flip it over and trim off excess fabric.

Now we'll insert piping at the left edge in a clever way, by facing the curved edge of the next section of fabric.

1. Cut both a new fabric strip and a new lining fabric as wide as you want.

2. Layer these two new pieces wrong sides together.

3. To cut the curved edge, overlap the first sewn-on piece, laying the double strip at least 1" inside its left raw edge.

4. Carefully cut a long series of curves along the right edge of these two new top fabrics the length of the underneath piece. Be careful not to cut any underneath fabrics or to cut away more than 1".

5. Remove this newly cut fabric and lining and place the lining on top of the outside fabric, right sides together.

6. Pin them together only at the cut, curved edges.

7. Sew these two pieces together using a 1/4" seam allowance, along the curved edges only.

8. Clip along the curved edges and turn right sides out.

9. Press. You have now made a curved, faced edge.

10. Pin this newly faced edge onto the base, overlapping the previously sewn edge about 1/2".

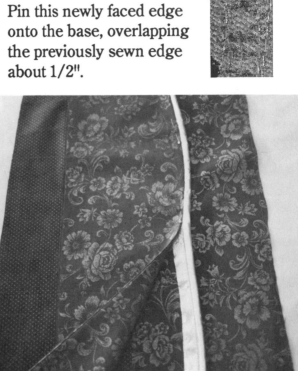

11. Next, slide the raw edges of the piping underneath the faced edge and pin in place (Fig. 3-40).

12. Put a zipper foot on the machine.

13. Thread needle with color to match fabric.

14. Topstitch close to the faced edge to catch all layers underneath, including the raw edges of the piping.

Fig. 3-40: Stay-stitch initial fabric onto cut-out garment lining edge. A faced curved section is turned, pressed, and placed over first section with gold lamé piping inserted along curved faced edge.

15. Repeat this method across the entire lining surface (Fig. 3-41).

16. Trim off excess fabric and piping from the wrong side of the beginning and ending edges.

Fig. 3-41: Completed piped edge on garment section.

17. Before sewing the garment's pieces together, remove piping cording from the seam allowances. The easiest method is to gently pull out the edge of the piping with either tweezers or surgical clamp scissors. The latter is available inexpensively in a medical supply store.

18. Pull the remaining piping back inside the piping casing by gently tugging the center section so that the cord returns to its original place. By removing the excess cording on the seam allowance, the excess bulk is also removed.

19. Finish the seams by either a serger or bias tape along the edges, or line the piece.

PIPED PATCHWORK

When piping is used in patchwork, all the pieces are dramatically framed and the results are spectacular. It almost has a textured, stained-glass effect. If done with thin lamé piping, the end results are worth the effort.

1. Cut out and piece the patchwork with a 1/4" seam allowance. Your piping should also have a 1/4" seam allowance to make it easier to stitch.

2. If you have made or purchased piping with a wider seam, trim off excess fabric to 1/4".

3. Pin the piping to one edge of one piece of patchwork, so that the outside raw edges are flush with the patchwork raw edges.

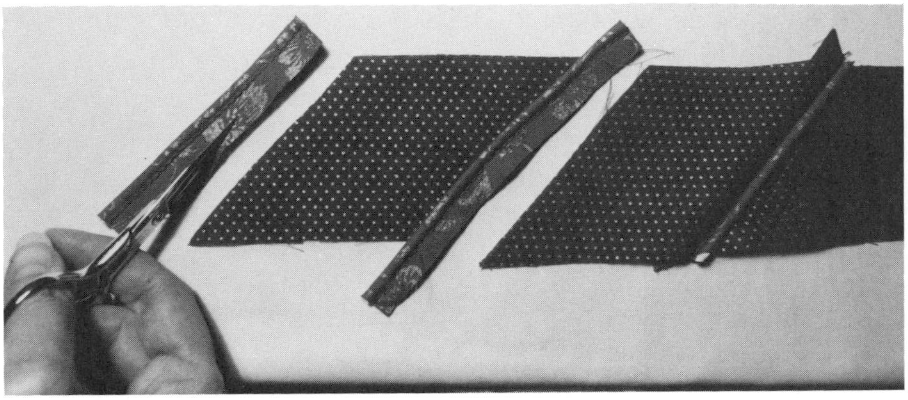

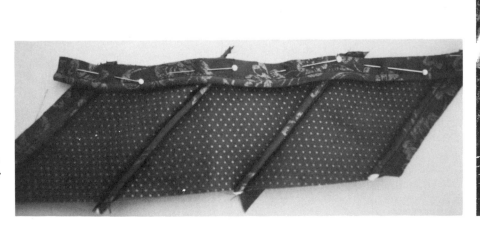

Fig. 3-42:
Trim
commercial
piping to 1/4"
and sew onto
edge of
patchwork
piece.

4. Stitch it in place before the next piece is sewn onto the piping (Fig. 3-42).

5. Turn the patchwork over and trim off the excess piping on the wrong side.

6. After you pipe the pieces initially, they can be sewn together as in regular piecing (Fig. 3-43).

7. Be sure to sew a piece of piping onto any inside or outside edges.

8. Then sew a long strip of piping onto one top edge of a patchwork row (Fig. 3-44). Thus, when the rows are sewn together, they will also be piped. Because the piping is thin, there is very little distortion when sewing the layers of piping together. You do not need to remove cording from the seam allowances as with larger piping (see Sectional Piping on page 132).

Fig. 3-43:
Sew unpiped
edge onto
piped edge.

Fig. 3-44:
When patch-
work row is
finished, pipe
edge with a
vertical piping
sewn on top of
the horizontal
row.

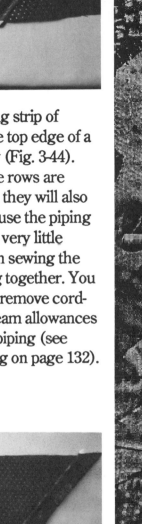

When quilting piped patchwork by machine, you may have trouble getting the presser foot over the piped sections, particularly the seams with more than one layer of piping. Try a darning or circular embroidery foot. You may still need to lift the presser foot slightly to ease by the patchwork as you are machine quilting. This works well with the knee-lift lever built into a Bernina sewing machine.

This type of piped patchwork can also be used with curved seams as well as straight seams. The bias in the piping makes it easy to turn along curved edges.

PIPED APPLIQUÉ

Machine-appliqué shapes can also be set off by using narrow piping. Again, using lamé piping can add just the right amount of glitz to a project.

1. Trace appliqué shape onto the wrong side of the appliqué fabric. You could use the motifs printed onto cotton fabrics, such as chintz roses, in which case the sewing line will be just **outside** the edge of the printing. Sewing **on** the printed motif edge will distort the whole motif after it is sewn.

2. Cut out the appliqué, leaving at least 1/2" extra around.

3. Place piece of fabric underneath, cut from the same fabric or a similar-colored fabric for best results.

4. Pin the two layers with right sides together.

5. Straight stitch on the appliqué line all the way around. Stitch 1/2" beyond the original stitching line to eliminate backstitching.

Fig. 3-45: Place a piece of piping under finished heart shape.

6. Now trim 1/8" beyond the sewn edge. This will eliminate a lot of clipping. The only places to be clipped are the inside corners and the edges of the outside points.

7. Carefully cut an opening on the wrong side of the sewn and clipped appliqué piece.

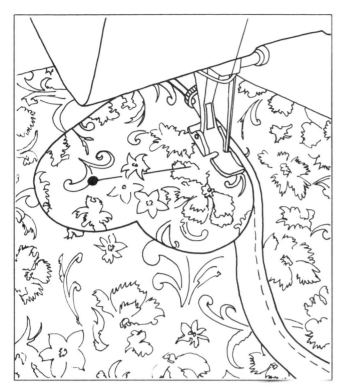

Fig. 3-46:
Straight stitch
piping with a
zipper foot
underneath
heart appliqué
shape.

edge of the appliqué, next to the piping (Fig. 3-46). Use a long pin and slide the piping underneath all curves and bends as you come to them. Leave the needle down in the fabric every time you stop sewing. This eliminates any fabric slippage and will create even stitching.

12. At the end of the appliqué, cut off 1" extra of piping.

13. Rip out some piping stitching and cut off excess piping cord so that the two ends of the cording will butt.

8. Turn piece through to the right side, and press so that the back edges are underneath.

9. Pin the appliqué piece onto the background at the center of the appliqué piece. Leave all edges free.

10. Slide piping raw edges underneath an edge (Fig. 3-45). Although you can pin first, it is easier to slide the raw edges of the piping underneath the appliqué as you sew.

11. Start stitching about 1" from the cut edge of the piping. Use a zipper foot and thread the machine with a thread that matches the appliqué. Straight stitch all layers around the

14. Fold under one short edge and fold this over the beginning of the piping stitching.

15. Restitch beside piping join to finish off appliqué (Fig. 3-47).

Fig. 3-47:
Completed
piped appliqué
shape.

Putting on the Glitz 4

HOW TO PATCHWORK A GARMENT SECTION

In this chapter you will learn how to make a patchwork section for a vest or jacket such as shown on the front cover. The same techniques will work for an accessory, such as a belt, detachable collar, or purse. First, you will make prairie points. Then you'll make checkerboards.

Generally, because of all the extra seams buy twice the amount of yardage specified in the pattern. If the garment calls for 3-1/2 yards, you will need about 6 to 7 yards total of the unusual fabrics and colors that will individualize your project.

The really fun part of this project will be collecting the fabrics. It may take some time to find a variety of coordinating fabrics and embellishments, but it's like a game to see where you find the most unusual or exciting components. From experience, we know what an adventure this can become. Sometimes it can take as long as six months to collect your materials. You look for something everywhere you go. When making these unusual purchases, other customers will ask what you are going to do. Of course, they think you are making a costume for a child's recital or a prom gown. When you explain, they look at you, think for a second, then tell you how pretty they think it will look. Take your time and enjoy this process.

Remember to buy fusibles in both white and black. Also, remember to buy threads. This may be trickier than you think because some stores carry only one brand of thread (see our Source List for mail-order companies). As you are collecting your fabrics, check each store for threads.

Remember your machine as well; stock up on needles. You may need several sizes to sew your fabrics and embellishments. Be sure you buy a variety.

Find your pattern, remembering the hints for pattern selection (see Chapter 2). To prepare the pattern for use, remove it from the package and separate the pieces you need from those you don't. Iron the paper pattern pieces with a

*Fig. 4-1:
This purse
shows how
prairie
points
can add
dimension
to a project.*

dry iron to make them flat.
Remember our recommendation to cut a muslin practice
piece and stitch it together first
to determine if the pattern fits
properly. Make any necessary
adjustments to the pattern.
Keep this muslin copy for
future use.

Before you begin to cut,
prepare your fabrics as directed for the fabric of
choice—refer to the Index for
the page number for your
fabric. For example, if you are
using tissue lamé, find the
subentry "fusing" listed on
pages 95–97. Turn to those
pages and you will read that
tissue lamé should be fused
before the cutting steps begin.
You may need to prewash your
fabric. If so, do it now and
check for colorfastness.

PRAIRIE POINTS

Once your fabric is prepared, cut several 4" squares of
fabric from one or several of
the fabrics. These will be used
to make prairie points. Prairie
points are folded fabric triangles that add a three-dimensional quality to your finished
piece when added to a seam or
surface. If made with a glitz
fabric, this quality is enhanced
by glitter and shine. The
number of squares needed will
range from five for a small
accessory (Fig. 4-1) to at least
three dozen for a jacket.

To make prairie points:

1. Fold the fabric in half on the
   grain, wrong sides together,
   and press flat with an iron.

2. Fold the outside folded
   corners down toward the
   center of the long raw edges,
   and press.

3. Straight stitch raw edges together on one side to hold, if desired (Fig. 4-2). Set these aside.

Fig. 4-2: Fold square in half and then fold each square from folded corner to the center of the bottom. Lay raw edge on seam between two layers of fabric to attach.

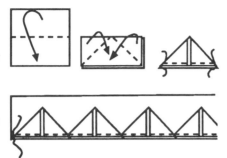

CHECKERBOARD

1. Cut remaining fabric in strips 1-1/2" and 2" wide.

2. Sew two strips of the same width but of different colors (light and dark) together along one long side, using a 1/4" scam allowance.

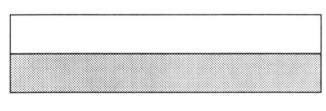

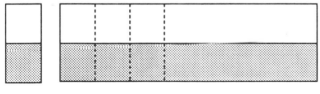

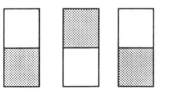

Fig. 4-3:
Fabric strips are stitched and then cut into segments and restitched as shown to form checkerboard patchwork.

3. Press seam allowances in one direction.

4. If the strips sewn are both 1-1/2" wide, cut across resulting strip in 1-1/2" increments.

5. Flip every other piece and sew back together to form a checkerboard strip (Fig. 4-3). Seams should meet with seam allowances lying in the opposite direction (Fig. 4-4).

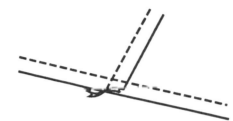

6. Press.

7. Sew one section after another without stopping until all sections are sewn and then cut apart between sections.

   Make at least five of these strips for a jacket. Set aside.

STRIP UNITS

1. From the remaining strips sew at least five different color strips together, using strips of the same size.

2. Cut this section apart in 3" increments (Fig. 4-5).

3. Turn the sections and sew the shorter raw edges together to form one long striped strip.

Fig. 4-4:
When sewing cut sections together, be sure seams meet in opposite directions.

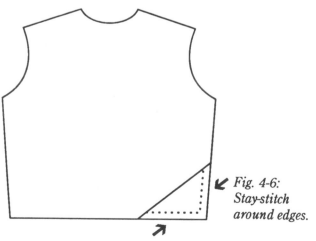

Fig. 4-5:
Sew five strips
together, then
cut apart.

4. Repeat the process and cut apart another increment, such as 1-1/2" or 2".

5. Make at least five of these strips in different widths for a jacket. Set aside.

FOUNDATION

1. Cut all garment sections from a foundation fabric that will not show through the patchwork, such as poly-cotton or muslin. Cut all sections an additional 1" beyond the original pattern edges. These will later be recut to the correct size.

2. On each of the garment sections, begin by choosing a wide strip for each bottom right corner. Stay-stitch these pieces 1/8" around

the outside edges to hold in place (Fig. 4-6). Trim off all excess fabric.

3. To make certain you cover the foundation fabric, lay any strip of fabric right side facing toward you next to the sewn corner strip (Fig. 4-7). Be sure that all the underneath fabric is

Fig. 4-6:
Stay-stitch
around edges.

*Fig. 4-7:
Place a fabric
strip on top,
right side up,
to see how it
looks.*

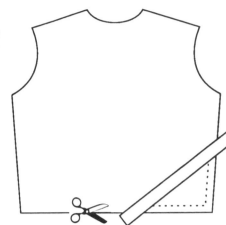

7. Now cut off excess end on
ironed strip (Fig. 4-9). Do
not cut any edges before they are
both sewn and ironed flat.

covered with the strip. Do
not cut off excess ends.

4. Flip it back onto the top
edge of the corner.

5. Sew along top seam in a 1/4"
seam allowance (Fig. 4-8).

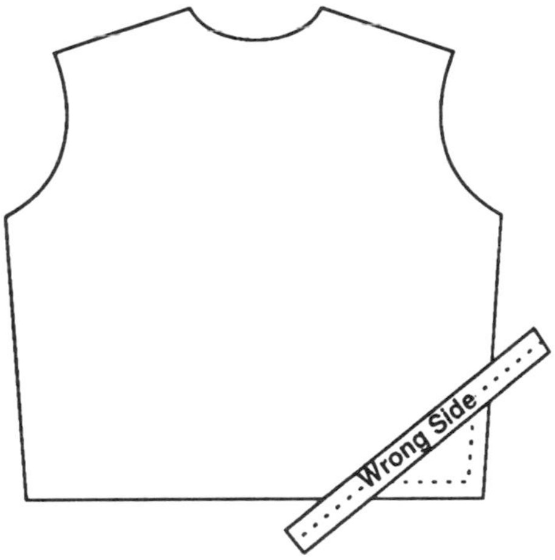

*Fig. 4-9:
Press strip up,
and trim off
excess.*

8. Repeat for next strip.

9. Now draw a line with a silver
Berol pencil diagonally
perpendicular to the last strip
across the left side on the
foundation fabric (Fig. 4-10).
This will mark the ending
line for the strips you are
adding.

10. As you continue adding
strips from the bottom right
upward, use the drawn line
as a stopping guide.

*Fig. 4-8:
Place strip
wrong side up
over previous
fabric piece
and stitch
across.*

6. Flip sewn strip back so that
the right side is facing you.
Press it flat with an iron
(depending on your fabric
content).

*Fig. 4-10:
Draw a
diagonal line
on opposite
side of
garment piece.*

11. Draw a second line parallel to the first line on the upper right, under the arm to the neck opening (Fig. 4-11).

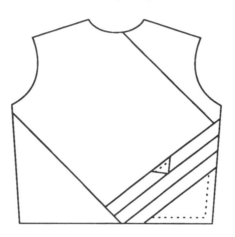

Fig. 4-11: Draw a line on upper right, under the arm to the neck opening. Add a prairie point as you go.

12. As you sew on the strips, add a prairie point along a few of the seams.

13. Pin prairie points with raw edges flush against the last sewn strip's raw edges.

14. Place a new strip over the pinned prairie point and sew along seam to catch all raw edges.

15. Repeat insertion of prairie points occasionally throughout. Be sure to add the checkerboard strips and the striped pieces occasionally.

16. Do not sew strips beyond drawn pencil lines.

17. Continue this until the center diagonal section of the section is covered with patchwork.

18. Now sew strips onto the two other sections, pinning and sewing the strips parallel to the pencil lines, from the centers toward the edges.

19. Continue with the strips, patchwork, and prairie points until the entire surface is covered (Fig. 4-12).

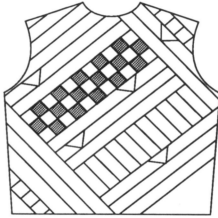

Fig. 4-12: Garment is now covered with patchwork.

20. If the garment is not to be quilted or batted, recut the patchwork section the exact size of the original pattern piece. If it is to be batted and quilted, cut batting the same size; machine or hand quilt.

21. After quilting, recut the sections using the original pattern, and construct the jacket as described in the chapter on selecting a pattern and as directed by the pattern instructions.

NOT QUITE AMISH QUILT
59"X59" WALL HANGING

Using lamés and other specialty fabrics and trims in quilts, quilted clothing, and patchwork projects can be exciting both during sewing and in the finished project. It is fun to anticipate what your project will look like throughout the process. The *Not Quite Amish* quilt (see color pages) was pieced and quilted by machine, making the whole process go by more quickly. If you have never tried machine quilting, or using specialty fabrics, you have all the information you need to begin right now.

If you prefer to make quilts, rather than garments, try using some of the materials and techniques mentioned in this book in your next creation. If you have never worked with unusual or specialty fabrics, introduce them to your quilts slowly.

For example, include lamé as one of the templates in a pieced pattern. To help, we have provided you with a pattern and some instructions for a quilt called *Not Quite Amish*.

But first, in case you're a beginner, here are some general instructions for making templates and piecing patchwork:

- To begin, transfer pattern pieces onto template material. Some people use cardboard cut from used cereal boxes, while others buy template plastic from quilt stores. Eventually, cardboard will wear down at the edges and become inaccurate.

- Transfer pattern name, block size, and cutting information onto each template. If seam allowance is included, be sure to add that to the information.

- In quilting, the seam allowance is 1/4". Some pattern sources give the patterns without seam allowances for hand piecing. In this case, the 1/4" is usually added to the template when the fabric is cut. Begin by drawing a pencil line around the template on the wrong side of your fabric. Experienced quilters eyeball the 1/4" excess beyond that piece before drawing the next piece, remembering that it, too, needs to have a 1/4" extra seam allowance. Others prefer to mark both the sewing line and the cutting line and use a 1/4" marker to make sure their lines are straight before cutting.

- Once you have prepared your templates, cut them out. Lay them on the wrong side of the fabric. If there is no seam allowance on the pieces, remember to leave space between the pieces when cutting. If the seam allowance is included on the template, pieces may be butted up against one another to save fabric. If many pieces of each template are to be cut, you might like to layer your fabrics to allow you to cut more than one piece at a time. Some templates need both a right and left side (or a reverse) when cutting. Simply flip the template over to make both the right and left piece.

- Some patterns do not require templates, but use cut fabric strips, which saves you a great deal of time in the cutting and piecing process. Strip piecing is the technique of cutting fabric strips across the width of the fabric and then stitching them together in sections. The sections are pressed, then cut into smaller segments. These are resewn into units, then larger units until the entire pattern is complete. (See Fig. 4-3).

- Strip widths are calculated by determining the desired width of the finished piece and adding 1/4" to each side (a total of 1/2" extra). Thus, a 2" cut strip would measure 1-1/2" after seaming.

There are many other methods for combining strips to create other shapes, with many books devoted to quick-cutting methods. Because this is not a quick-piecing book, we will not go into these methods.

Once your pieces are cut, follow the piecing or appliqué instructions given with your pattern for putting the units together. Usually pieces are assembled into units, the units into blocks, and the blocks into a top. The pattern for the quilt given here uses this method for assembly.

When you finish the center portion of the top, add borders; then choose a quilting design and mark the top with a water-erasable marker. Next sandwich the batting between the backing and the top. To hold these layers together and keep them from moving during the quilting process, you may baste the layers together by hand or safety pin the layers with #1 safety pins every 6". Quilting can be done by hand using a hoop or a frame, or by machine. Because this book recommends machine methods, the instructions with our pattern are for machine quilting.

When the quilting is complete, remove the pins or basting stitches. Trim the edges even and finish them. The usual finishing method is to apply bias binding to the front and turn it to the back, then stitch it in place by hand. Other finishing methods include folding the front to the back or the back to the front and stitching in place. When the quilt is complete, it should be signed and dated. It might need a sleeve on the back top edge if it is to be hung on the wall.

ALTERNATE DESIGNS

The design for the quilt *Not Quite Amish*, done on a Macintosh computer, was fun to work with. With the drawing capabilities of the graphics program, it is possible to take a 6" basic unit like the one shown in Figure 4-13 and duplicate it over and over. Once it has been duplicated, it can be moved around in different locations to produce an overall design. It is possible to save that design and start with the unit again and make an-

other. Notice Figures 4-14 and 4-15 on the next pages. Figure 4-14 is the layout of the quilt as it is shown in the completed piece. Before the actual quilt was constructed, we printed several copies of the design and colored them in to test the placement of the colors.

Figure 4-15 is an alternate choice for laying out the units. We colored it in with colored pencils as well, but it wasn't the best choice, and we set it aside to try at another time. We still had plenty of time to play with the unit further. Look at Figure 4-16. It shows the same unit with triangle/ squares placed at the corners. These units provide different designs when placed with four or more others at different angles (Figs. 4-17 a–c on page 150). The resulting designs provide food for thought and more ideas for other quilts. We are sharing these drawings with you in hopes that you will make copies of them and color them with your own favorite colors. Think about using lamés and other specialty fabrics to liven up your quilt.

Not Quite Amish uses Amish colors, but the use of the gold lamé makes it impossible to be an Amish quilt.

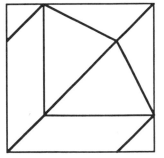

Fig. 4-13: Basic 6" unit used to make Not Quite Amish *quilt*.

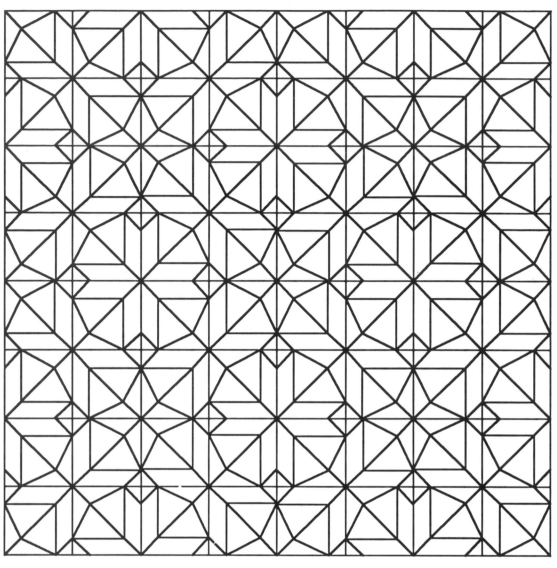

MATERIALS NEEDED

1-1/2 yards each, purple and burgundy

2 yards gold lamé

1 yard magenta

2-1/2 yards black

4 yards woven cotton fusible

2 spools metallic thread

1 spool sewing thread

batting 64" x 64" (purchase a 72" x 90" and cut to size)

4 yards backing fabric

rotary cutter, mat, scissors, template material, water-erasable marker, 1" safety pins

INSTRUCTIONS

1. Prepare templates as directed on pattern pieces (Fig. 4-18). Cut from fabric as directed on the templates.

2. You will need 64 units to complete the top. This results in a 48"-square completed top before borders. Construct these units in three different color combinations. Make four units of combination #1: C pieces in black, D triangles in burgundy, B pieces in magenta, and A pieces in gold lamé. Make 32 units of combination #2: A pieces in gold lamé, B pieces in black, and C and D pieces in burgundy. Make 28 units of combination #3: A in purple, B in magenta, C in black, and D in burgundy. Sew templates as follows: Piece D to C and add B and A.

Fig. 4-15:
An alternate
layout design
for use of the
same unit.

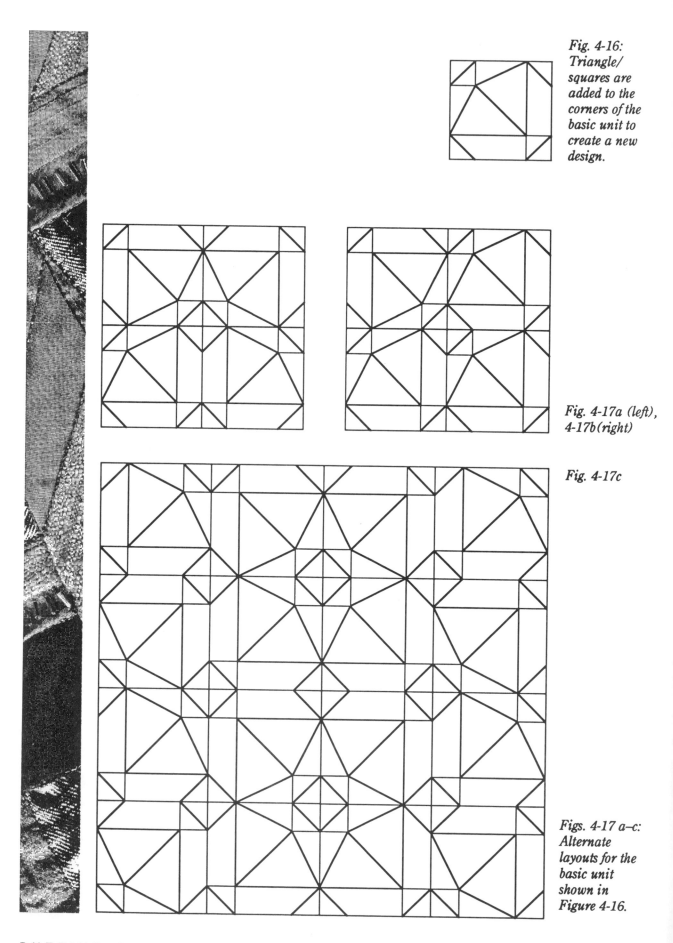

Fig. 4-16:
Triangle/
squares are
added to the
corners of the
basic unit to
create a new
design.

Fig. 4-17a (left),
4-17b (right)

Fig. 4-17c

Figs. 4-17 a–c:
Alternate
layouts for the
basic unit
shown in
Figure 4-16.

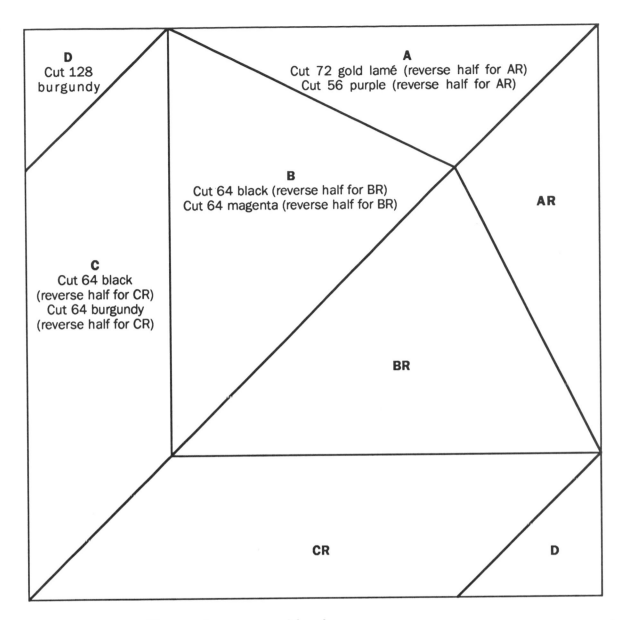

D
Cut 128
burgundy

A
Cut 72 gold lamé (reverse half for AR)
Cut 56 purple (reverse half for AR)

B
Cut 64 black (reverse half for BR)
Cut 64 magenta (reverse half for BR)

AR

C
Cut 64 black
(reverse half for CR)
Cut 64 burgundy
(reverse half for CR)

BR

CR

D

Repeat for reverse side of the unit and sew together down the center to complete the 6" unit.

3. Once you have completed all of the units, place them in rows using Figure 4-19 as a guide. Sew together in rows and then sew rows together to complete the top. Press top. The completed pieced section of your top should now measure 48" x 48".

4. Add border strips to the completed top, mitering the corners where directed, to make a larger-size quilt. You can cut the strips longer to allow extra for miter, since excess is trimmed off when miter is complete (measurements given are exact size) (Fig. 4-20 a). Cut four of the first black border strips 2" x 52-1/2". Add to quilt top, mitering corners as shown in Figure 4-20 a, b, and c. Cut

Fig. 4-18: Full-size pattern. Use to make templates for each piece.

four strips for the next border from gold lamé 1-1/2" x 52-1/2". Add two strips to opposite sides. Sew two small purple squares 1-1/2" x 1-1/2" to the ends of each of the remaining strips before adding them to the two remaining sides of the top. Cut four black strips

3-1/2" x 59-1/2" for final border and add to all four sides, mitering the corners. Press top.

To miter corners, cut strips the length of the side to which the border strips are being added plus twice the width of the strips, with a 1/4" seam

Fig. 4-19: Placement diagram.

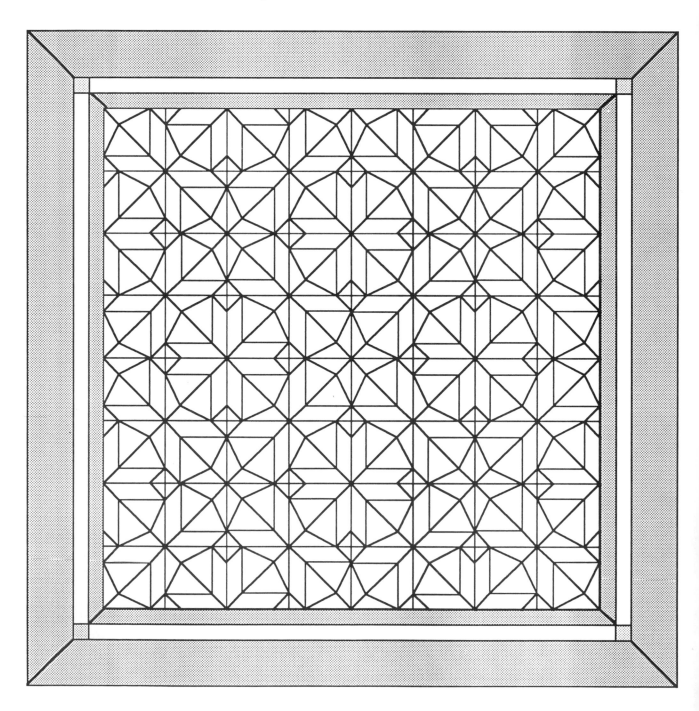

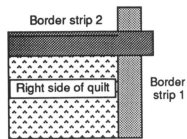

Fig. 4-20a: Mitering.

allowance added for each seam (total 1/2"). For example, to add a 2" mitered border to a 24" square you would cut your strips 28-1/2" for each side. Remember, the strips may be cut longer to guarantee enough length—the excess may be trimmed off after mitering is complete. To be sure you place the strip on the piece properly, mark the center of the strip and the center of the constructed piece and pin together from that point to the corners. Sew strips to each side, starting and stopping 1/4" from ends. When all four border strips have been added, start mitering at one corner by folding one strip over the other at a 45-degree angle and press (Fig. 4-20 b). You may

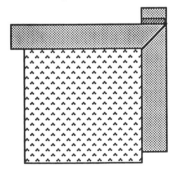

Fig. 4-20b: Mitering.

slipstitch the angle in place by hand and trim away the excess on the back and press seam

open. If corner miter is stitched by machine, turn quilt top to wrong side. At the corner, fold border strips back at a 45-degree angle and press. Pick up the quilt top and fold on the diagonal so border strips extend and match the crease lines made during pressing (Fig. 4-20 c). Stitch on the crease line beginning at the outside edge and working in toward the quilt. Be sure to backstitch at the begin-

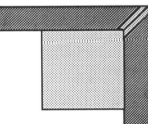

ning and the end. Trim off excess fabric and press seam open to finish (Fig. 4-20 d). Repeat for all four corners (Fig. 4-20 e).

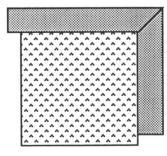

Fig. 4-20c: Mitering.

Fig. 4-20d: Mitering.

Fig. 4-20e: Mitering.

5. Decide on the quilting pattern. The quilt shown was machine quilted in the seams and 1/4" outside each seam around all the pieces using gold metallic thread. If you will be using a design that requires marking, mark on the quilt top with a water-erasable marker now.

6. Once you have prepared the top for quilting, sandwich the batting between the top and the prepared backing. Pin layers together with #1 safety pins from center out every 6". Be sure quilt is flat with no wrinkles or puckers.

7. Start quilting in the center and work your way to the outside. To begin quilting, stitch several stitches in place to lock the threads. End in the same manner. Plan your starts and stops to keep them to a minimum.

8. When quilting is complete, trim off threads. Trim edges even and bind with self-made bias binding (see instructions in bias section) to finish. Add a sleeve to hang and sign and date the back.

Congratulations! You've finished your quilt.

CONCLUSION

Using the information you have gleaned from reading this book, and the skills you have acquired through becoming familiar with your sewing machine, you are ready to try new fabrics, threads, and techniques. You may meet with some failures along the way, but don't give up; your end results will be worth all of your efforts. Try to envision your finished project before you start and make goals for yourself that can be achieved along the way to completion.

As you are "Putting on the Glitz" on your next project, we hope that you can refer to this book for help along the way. We look forward to seeing your work in our future travels.

SOURCE LIST

The following is a list of good mail-order sources for equipment, materials, embellishments, and supplies. Regardless of where you live, your choices should not be limited to what is available in your area. Just sit down with a pen and paper (or telephone) and contact the company or business you want from this list. Many of them have free catalogs or helpful brochures to help you make your decisions.

BATTING

Fairfield Processing, P.O. Box 1130, Danbury, CT 06813. *Polyester and blend battings and stuffings.*

Heartfelt, Box 1829, Vineyard Haven, MA 02568. *100% wool batting.*

Hobbs Bonded Fibers, 345 Owen Lane, Suite 114, Waco, TX 76710. *Send SASE for information about their polyester batting.*

Stearns Technical Textiles Company, Mountain Mist Consumer Products, 100 Williams St., Cincinnati, OH 45215-6316. (800) 345-7150. *Manufacturers of both polyester and 100% cotton battings.*

Taos Mountain Wool Works, P.O. Box 327, Arroyo Hondo, NM 87513. (505) 776-2925. *Wool battings.*

Warm Products, Inc., 11232 120th NE #112, Kirkland, WA 98033. (800) 234-WARM. *Manufacturers of Warm & Natural batting.*

YLI Corp., 482 N Freedom Blvd., Provo, UT 84601. *Suppliers of silk batting, novelty threads for sewing, serging, and embroidery. Catalog $1.50.*

SEWING MACHINES

Bernina of America, Inc., 534 W. Chestnut, Hinsdale, IL 60521. *Sewing machines, sergers, Create-A-Space Table.*

Elna, Inc., 7642 Washington Ave. S., Minneapolis, MN 55344. *Sewing machines, sergers, pressing machines.*

Fox Sewing Machines, Inc., 307 W. 38th St., New York, NY 10018. *Sells and repairs industrial sewing equipment. Sells steam irons and cutting machines.*

New Home Sewing Co., 100 Hollister Rd., Teterboro, NJ 07608. *Sewing machines, Janome silk threads.*

Pfaff American Sales Corp., 610 Winters Ave., Paramus, NJ 07653. *Sewing machines and sergers.*

Singer Sewing Co., 200 Metroplex Dr., Edison, NJ 08818. *Sewing machines, presses, overlock machines.*

VWS, Inc., 11760 Berea Road, Cleveland, OH 44111-1601. *Both Viking and White sewing machines, sergers, and presses.*

CUTTING TABLES

Bernina of America, Inc. *See Sewing Machines, above.*

Daynell, 1017 S. W. Morrison, Portland, OR 97205. (800) 222-5106. *Folding cardboard table.*

Sew/Fit Company, P.O. Box 565 Lagrange, IL 60525. *Folding cardboard table.*

PATTERNS

Burda Patterns, P.O. Box 2517, Smyrna, GA 30081. *European patterns.*

Fashion Blueprints, 2191 Blossom Valley Dr., San Jose, CA 95124. *Ethnic patterns.*

Folkwear Patterns, P.O. Box 355, Newtown, CT 06470-9989. *Recently bought by* Threads Magazine. *Ethnic patterns.*

Great Fit Patterns, 221 SE 197th Ave., Portland, OR 97233. *Women's patterns size 38–60.*

Kwik Sew Pattern Co., 3000 Washington Ave. North, Minneapolis, MN 55411. *Patterns.*

Marge Murphy Heirloom Quilting Designs, P.O. Box 6306, Biloxi, MS 39532. *Patterns, silk batting.*

Stretch and Sew Patterns, P.O. Box 185, Eugene, OR 97440. *Patterns, knits, and interfacings.*

That Patchwork Place, Inc., P.O. Box 118, Bothell, WA 98041. *Quilting books and patterns.*

INTERFACING

Dritz Corp., P.O. Box 5028, Spartanburg, SC 29304. *Interfacings and other sewing notions.*

HTC-Hendler Textile Corp., Consumer Products Division, 450 7th Ave., New York, NY 10123. *Interfacings.*

J & R Interfacings, c/o Dritz Corp., P.O. Box 5028, Spartanburg, SC 29304. *Interfacings and specialty fabrics.*

Pellon Company Limited Partnership, Consumer Products Dept., 119 W. 40th St., New York, NY 10018. (212)391-6300. *Interfacings.*

Staple Sewing Aids, 141 Lanza Ave., Garfield, NJ 07026. (800)631-3820. *Interfacings.*

NOTIONS AND SUPPLIES

Aardvark Adventures, Box 2449, Livermore, CA 94550. *Glitz threads, beads, shishas, creative books. Catalog $1.00.*

B&J Fabrics, 263 W. 40th St., New York, NY 10018. *Unusual novelty fabrics. Mail order, $15 minimum.*

Bazaar Del Mundo, 2754 Calhoun St., San Diego, CA 92110. *Shisha mirrors, unusual trims and fabrics.*

Cabin Fever Calicos, P.O. Box 550106, Atlanta, GA 30355. *Quilt books, notions, fabrics, batting.*

Celtic Design Company, 834 West Remington Drive, Sunnyvale, CA 94087. *Bias bars.*

Clotilde, Inc., 1909 SW First Ave., Ft. Lauderdale, FL 33315. *Threads, books, videos, needles, pins, notions, Ultrasuede scraps, generic sewing machine feet. Catalog available for $1.*

Coats & Clark, 30 Patewood Drive, Suite 351, Greenville, SC 29615. Attention: Meta Hoge. *Write for retail sales locations or consumer information.*

Dorr Mill Store, P.O. Box 88, Guild, NH 03754-0088. *100% wool in solid colors. $3 for two color charts.*

Dover Street Booksellers, P.O. Box 1563, 39 E. Dover St., Easton, MD 21601. *Extensive selection of books.*

Exotic Silks, 252 State St., Los Altos, CA 94022. *Silks. Complete set of swatches $20; if swatches returned in a month, $18 refunded.*

The Fabric Carr, P.O. Box 32120, San Jose, CA 95152. (415) 948-7373. *Professional ironing supplies, sewing notions, books.*

G Street Fabrics, 11854 Rockville Pike, Rockville, MD 20852. *All fabrics mail order, custom service. $2 swatch service.*

Gladstone Fabrics, 16 W. 56th St., New York, NY 10019. *Metallic brocades, sequined fabrics, and more. Supplies for theatrical costumes. Mail order with $10 minimum.*

Gordon Button Co., Inc., 142 W. 38th St., New York, NY 10018. *Buttons, ornaments, and buckles.*

Greenberg & Hammer, Inc., 24 W. 57th St., New York, NY 10019. (212) 246-2835. *Notions, patterns, silk threads, scissors, professional irons and more. Mail-order catalog, $15 minimum.*

The Hands Work, P.O. Box 386, Pecos, NM 87552. *Handmade and washable buttons. $2 catalog.*

Hersh 6th Avenue Buttons, Inc., 1000 6th Ave., New York, NY 10018. (212) 391-6615. *Large selection of dressmaking, millinery notions, and tools.*

Jehlor Fantasy Fabrics, 17900 South Center Pkwy. Suite 290, Seattle, WA 98188. *Lamé, trims, beads, and sequins. $2.50 for catalog.*

Keepsake Quilting, P.O. Box 1459, Meredith, NH 03253. *Books, notions, fabrics, lamé samples, batting.*

Kieffer's Lingerie Supplies, 1625 Hennepin Ave., Minneapolis, MN 55403. *Notions, lingerie fabrics, lace, notions.*

Lacis, 2990 Adeline, Berkeley, CA 94703. *New and antique laces. $1.50 for catalog.*

M&J Trimming Company, 1008 6th Ave., New York, NY 10018. (212)391-9072. *Huge selection of trims and embellishments. Mail order with $50 minimum.*

Madeira USA Ltd., 30 Bayside Ct., Laconia, NH 03247-6068. *High quality threads, yarns, and flosses.*

Nancy's Notions, Ltd., P.O. Box 683, Beaver Dam, WI 53916. *Books, videos, notions, fabrics, fusibles. Free catalog.*

Newark Dressmaker Supply, Box 2448, Lehigh Valley, PA 18001. (215)837-7500. *Mail-order source for almost all sewing supplies. Free catalog.*

Lew Novik, Inc., 45 W. 38th St., New York, NY 10018. *Large selection of metallic novelty fabrics, laces, ribbons, and more.*

The Perfect Notion, 566 Hoyt St., Darien, CT 06820. *Notions.*

Poli Fabrics, 132 W. 57th St., New York, NY 10019. (212) 245-7589. *Almost all natural-fiber fabrics.*

Yvonne Porcella Studios, 3619 Shoemake Ave., Modesto, CA 95351. *Pieced clothing, printed clothing, variations, jacket patterns. SASE for information.*

Quilters' Resource, Inc., P.O. Box 148850, Chicago, IL. 60614. *Lamés, all types of threads and glitz supplies.*

QuiltSmith, Ltd., 252 Cedar Road, Poquoson, VA 23662. *ARDCO metal templates and rulers. SASE for catalog.*

Rosen and Chadick, 246 W. 40th St., New York, NY 10018. *Imported and designer fabrics, bridal, lace, velvets, lamé, and more.*

Margaret Schwanck, 7642 Washington Ave. South, Eden Prairie, MN 55344. *Ribbon floss.*

Sew Art International, P.O. Box 550, Bountiful, UT 84010. *Invisible thread, other unusual threads.*

Sheru Enterprises, Inc., 49 W. 38th St., New York, NY 10018. (212) 730-0766. *Supplies for crafts, beading, macramé, sew-on and glue-on jewels, sequins, and more. Mail order with a $35 minimum. Catalog.*

So-Good, Inc., 28 W. 38th St., New York, NY 10018. (212)398-0236. *This store sells all sorts of ribbons and trims. Mail-order catalog, $25 minimum.*

Speed Stitch, 3113 Broadpoint Drive, Harbor Heights, FL 33983. *Sulky metallic threads, invisible threads, Sulky rayon threads, machine embroidery supplies. Catalog $3 (refundable with purchase).*

Steinlauf and Stoller, Inc., 239 W. 39th St., New York, NY 10018. (800)637-1637. *Large selection of threads, snaps, trims, tools, interfacings, and more. $30 minimum or $5 service charge.*

Marinda Stewart, P.O. Box 402, Walnut Creek, CA 94596. *Specialty garment patterns, punch-needle books.*

Swiss-Metrosene, Inc., 1107 Marlin Dr., Roseville, CA 95661. *Threads.*

June Tailor, Inc., P.O. Box 208, Richfield, WI 53076. *Pressing and ironing equipment.*

Things Japanese, 9805 NE 116th St., Kirkland, WA 98034. *Tire silk twist and other specialty threads.*

L.P. Thur Designer Fabrics, 126 W. 23rd St., New York, NY 10011. *Large selection of spandex and budget fabrics. Mail order with $20 minimum.*

Tinsel Trading Co., 47 W. 38th St., New York, NY 10018. (212)730-1030. *A wonderful store to find antique gold and silver trims. Also sells real gold and silver threads. Mail order with $25 minimum.*

Treadleart, 25834 Narbonne Ave., Lomita, CA 90717. *Decorative and utility machine threads.*

Trebor Textiles, 251A W. 39th St., New York, NY 10018. *Designer fabrics at discount prices. Sells mail order. No minimum.*

William Wawak Co., Box 59281, Schaumberg, IL 60159-0281. *Tailors' supplies, interfacings, linings, thread, leather, and more.*

BIBLIOGRAPHY

BOOKS AND ARTICLES

Allen, Alice. "Simply Serging," *Quick & Easy Quilting*, Fall, 1990. House of White Birches.

Bernina Special. Bernina of America, 1983.

Brown, Gail. *Sensational Silk.* Palmer/Pletsch,

Brown, Gail, and Tammy Young. *Innovative Sewing.* Chilton, 1990.

Bullard, Lacy Folmar, and Betty Jo Shiell. *Chintz Quilts: Unfading Glory.* Serendipity Publishers, 1983.

The Complete Book of Sewing. Greystone Corporation, 1972.

Delaney-Mech, Susan, "Rx for Quilters," *Quilt World*, Dec./Jan. 1989. House of White Birches.

Denner, Linda. *The Grand Finale.* American Quilter's Society, 1988.

Dittman, Margaret. *The Fabric Lover's Scrapbook.* Chilton, 1988.

Dodson, Jackie. *Know Your Sewing Machine* series. Chilton, 1988.

Fanning, Robbie and Tony. *The Complete Book of Machine Quilting.* Chilton, 1980.

Gross, Nancy D., and Frank Fontana. *Shisha Embroidery.* Dover Publications, 1981.

Hargrave, Harriet. *Heirloom Machine Quilting.* Burdett Publications, 1987.

Herbort, Diane E., and Susan Greenhut. *The Quiltwear Book.* EPM Publications, 1988.

Johannah, Barbara. *The Quick Quiltmaking Handbook.* Pride of the Forest, 1979.

Krohn, Margaret B., and Phyllis W. Schwebke. *How to Sew Leather, Suede, Fur.* Bruce Publishing, 1966.

Mashuta, Mary. *Wearable Art for Real People.* C & T Publishing, 1989.

McCauley, Daniel and Kathryn. *Decorative Arts of the Amish of Lancaster County.* Good Books, 1988.

Montano, Judith. *The Crazy Quilt Handbook.* C & T Publishing, 1986.

Montgomery, Florence M.. *Textiles in America 1650-1870.* W. W. Norton, 1984.

Moore, Dorothy. *Pattern Drafting and Dressmaking.* Western Publishing, 1971.

Palmer, Pati, Gail Brown, and Sue Green. *Creative Serging Illustrated.* Chilton, 1987.

Palmer, Pati, and Susan Pletsch. *Easy, Easier, Easiest Tailoring.* Palmer/Pletsch, 1980.

Penders, Mary Coyne. *Color and Cloth.* Quilt Digest Press, 1989.

Pettit, Florence H. *America's Printed and Painted Fabrics.* Hastings House, 1970.

Quilting by Machine. Singer Sewing Reference Library, Cy de Cosse, Inc., 1990.

Saunders, Jan. *A Step-by-Step Guide to Your Sewing Machine.* Chilton, 1990.

Sewing Velvet from J.B. Martin Velvets.

Shaeffer, Claire. *Claire Shaeffer's Fabric Sewing Guide.* Chilton, 1989.

Simplicity Sewing Book. Simplicity Pattern Co., 1979.

Singer Sewing Essentials. Singer Sewing Reference Library, Cy de Cosse, Inc., 1984.

Smith, Lois. *Fun & Fancy Machine Quiltmaking.* American Quilter's Society, 1989.

Superstar/A Decade of Design. Fairfield Processing Corp., 1988.

Tailoring. Singer Sewing Reference Library, Cy de Cosse, Inc., 1989.

Wells, Jean. *A Patchworthy Apparel Book.* Yours Truly, Inc., 1981.

Wells, Jean. *Fans.* C & T Publishing, 1987.

Wingate, Isabel B. *Textile Fabrics and Their Selection.* Prentice-Hall, 1964.

PERIODICALS AND NEWSLETTERS

Butterick Sewing World, Butterick Co., 161 Ave. of the Americas, New York, NY 10013.

Handwoven, Interweave Press, 201 E. 4th St., Loveland, CO 80537.

McCall's Patterns, The McCall Pattern Co., 230 Park Ave., New York, NY 10169.

Professional Quilter, Box 75277, St. Paul, MN 55175.

Quilter's Newsletter Magazine, P.O. Box 394, Wheatridge, CO 80034-0394.

Quilt World, Quick & Easy Quilting, Stitch N' Sew Quilts, House of White Birches, 306 East Parr Road, Berne, IN 46711.

Sew Beautiful, 518 Madison St., Huntsville, AL 35801-4286.

Sewer's SourceLetter, CraftSource, 7509 7th Place SW, Seattle WA 98106.

Sew News, PJS Publications, Inc., P.O. Box 1790, News Plaza, Peoria, IL 61656.

Simplicity Today, 200 Madison Ave., New York, NY 10016.

Threads Magazine, Taunton Press, Box 5506, Newtown, CT 06470-5506.

Update Newsletters, 2269 Chestnut # 269, San Francisco, CA 94123.

Vogue Patterns, 161 Ave. of the Americas, New York, NY 10013.

INDEX